Exemplars of Curriculum Theory

Arthur K. Ellis
Seattle Pacific University

EYE ON EDUCATION
6 DEPOT WAY WEST, SUITE 106
LARCHMONT, NY 10538
(914) 833–0551
(914) 833–0761 fax
www.eyeoneducation.com

Library of Congress Cataloging-in-Publication Data

Ellis, Arthur K.
    Exemplars of curriculum theory / Arthur K. Ellis.
        p. cm.
    Includes bibliographical references and index.
    ISBN 1-930556-70-5
        1. Education--Curricula--United States. 2. Curriculum planning--Social aspects--United States. I. Title.

LB1570.E44 2004
375'.001--dc22   2003059555

10 9 8 7 6 5

Editorial and production services provided by
Richard H. Adin Freelance Editorial Services
52 Oakwood Blvd., Poughkeepsie, NY 12603-4112
(914-471-3566)

Also Available
from EYE ON EDUCATION

Research on Educational Innovations, 3/e
Arthur K. Ellis

**Instructional Supervision:
Applying Tools and Concepts**
Sally J. Zepeda

The Principal As Instructional Leader
Sally J. Zepeda

School Community Relations
Douglas J. Fiore

**School Leader Internship: Developing, Monitoring,
and Evaluating Your Leadership Experience**
Gary E. Martin, William F. Wright, and Arnold B. Danzig

**Introduction to Educational Administration
Standards, Theories, and Practice**
Douglas J. Fiore

**Human Resources Administration:
A School-Based Perspective, 2/e**
Richard E. Smith

Money and Schools, 2/e
David C. Thompson and R. Craig Wood

**What Great Principals Do Differently:
15 Things That Matter Most**
Todd Whitaker

Achievement Now!
Donald Fielder

**From Rigorous Standards to Student Achievement:
A Practical Process**
Rettig, McCullough, Watson, and Santos

About the Author

Arthur K. Ellis, a former public school teacher, is Director of the International Center for Curriculum Studies and Professor of Education at Seattle Pacific University. He is the author of the highly acclaimed *Teaching and Learning Elementary Social Studies, Seventh Edition* (Allyn and Bacon), *Research on Educational Innovations, Third Edition* and *Teaching, Learning, and Assessment Together* (both Eye On Education). Dr. Ellis is the author or coauthor of 18 published books and numerous journal articles. He consults to school systems in the United States and is involved in a wide range of professional activities in Russia, China, Spain, and other countries. He is also the coauthor of "Journeys of Discovery," an integrated studies curriculum for schools.

Acknowledgments

I wish to acknowledge the help of several individuals who made the book better than it might have been. Thanks to James Mikkelson and Daniel Freeborn of Colegio Americano de Madrid for their contributions to the material on the Diploma Programme of the International Baccalaureate Curriculum. Thanks to Darby Cavin of the English Department of Grays Harbor College for his contributions to the Foxfire and Sudbury Schools Curriculum material. And a special word of thanks to Naomi Petersen of Indiana University, South Bend, for her editorial diligence and for making crucial suggestions and additions to the text. I accept full responsibility for any omissions, errors, and other shortcomings that might be found in these pages.

Table of Contents

Introduction

Exemplar (noun). One that serves as model or example as (a) an ideal model (b) a typical or standard specimen.

Webster's Eleventh New Collegiate Dictionary (2003)

The purpose of this book is to acquaint you with models and exemplars of curriculum theory. A theory is an attempt to explain a phenomenon or phenomena in abstract terms and general principles. A theory typically contains a number of interrelated propositions, for example, "all children want to learn," or "students should study those things that interest them most." Theories of education tend to fall into two broad categories that we might call, traditional and experiential, for want of better terms. Two main theories, essentialism and progressivism, are explicated at some length. Other theories such as perennialism and existentialism, are dealt with more briefly simply because they play comparatively minor roles. A theory is a set of abstract principles about something, in this case, the proper education of the young. The term "philosophy" is often used to mean the coherent expression of a world view, and it is common to call essentialism, for example, an educational philosophy. However, I prefer to use the term theory to describe these abstract sets of principles because they are in fact, based on something more than metaphysical speculation. Essentialism and progressivism can each point to a long line of empirical studies to shore up their respective cases.

The models of curriculum I have chosen are three: learner-centered, society-centered, and knowledge-centered. A model is a selective representation of something, often compromising elements of space, time, and complexity. In other words, a model is a simplified version of some reality, for example, a map, a simulation, a schematic, or a working miniature. A useful model gives insight to reality without being the reality itself. Often, the key to a model's usefulness lies in the careful selection of relevant elements of the reality it represents. I have tried to be true to the models. In our case, the three models chosen are links between theory and exemplar. Whereas the theory sets forth general principles, the model explains and illustrates how the theory works.

It is important to note that realities are not often clear cut. This is so precisely because they are real and models are ideal. Therefore, you will note that none of the exemplars included are purely learner-, society-, or knowledge-centered. Rather, they have their tendencies, and I have attempted to place them appropriately. Consider the *Foxfire* curriculum for a moment. Of course, it is a curriculum that explores history, culture, geography, and language. But it is also oriented toward the local and regional society with a great deal of community involvement. And it accommodates the individual, particularly with regard to learner interest and freedom of choice. Similar comments could be made about the other exemplars, although more so in some cases than in others as you will see.

The exemplars are instances or specific cases. Exemplars offer specimens or particular instances of the models. They serve as concrete attempts to put the models into practice. The exemplars I have chosen as representative of the spirit of the models are the Exploratory Experiences Curriculum for Elementary Schools (EECES), Unified Science and Mathematics for Elementary Schools (USMES), E. D. Hirsch Jr's Core Knowledge Curriculum, the Sudbury Valley Schools Curriculum, Reggio Emilia education, the Foxfire Curriculum, the International Baccalaureate Curriculum, and Mortimer Adler's Paideia Proposal Curriculum.

Often a particular movement identifies itself by what it is *not.* All too often, this is done as part of a "straw man" argument, something John Dewey lamented about the progressive movement in his book, *Experience and Education.* Typically, other approaches are caricatured and demeaned, even lampooned, as irrelevant, unchallenging, inert, and/or superficial in contrast to the touted approach, which is, of course, relevant, challenging, alive, and supportive of life-long learning. This doesn't get us very far. What I have attempted to do is to present theories, models, and exemplars for what they claim to offer. I have made no attempt to tell you how deficient they might be. I truly believe that the reader is quite capable of making informed judgments regarding the appropriateness of curriculum to situation. Each of the curriculums illustrated has much to offer. If I thought it did not, I would not have included it. Often the difference in the appropriateness of a given curriculum depends on what one views as the purpose(s) of school. I know of no empirical evidence to cite "proving" that any one of the curriculums is significantly more capable of promoting the goals of schooling than any other.

There are two prominent goals of schooling: raising academic achievement and deepening the social/moral fabric. I have concluded that each of the curriculums presented in these pages is capable of doing that. This is so because a curriculum comes to life in the hands of teachers and students. It is in this very human encounter that good things happen. In that sense there is no such thing as a curriculum apart from the way things are in school life. Even the most noble curriculum can be rendered lifeless in the wrong hands. And school subjects that students typically tend to dislike suddenly become favorites in the right hands.

The theories, models, and exemplars of curriculum theory into practice that I have chosen as illustrative are somewhat arbitrary, to be sure. Anyone who has examined more than one curriculum text knows that the term "model" is variably used and that literally dozens of "models" have been written about and explained at length. I chose the three models included in this book because I think they represent the three most basic worldviews of what the curriculum is or ought to be. To the extent that I have represented them faithfully, the reader will find them a useful port of entry. The models are certainly subject to individual interpretation, as they should be, and they can and have been advocated along continuums from conservative to radical.

The exemplars, of which there are literally hundreds, were more difficult to select merely from the point of view of which to leave in and which to leave out. I do think that those that are presented in some depth (others are mentioned and briefly described along the way) furnish readers with the characteristic attributes and spirit of the enterprise, allowing them to seek out or develop other exemplars that represent adaptations, combinations, and permutations of the essence of each. It should be noted early on that no single exemplar is purely this or purely that. Theories and models may have pristine qualities that set them clearly apart from anything else, although even that idea is open to dispute. Readers will note that each of the exemplars illustrated in this book contains trace elements of other worldviews. This is so because they are real curriculums to be used in real educational settings. Realities are inevitably somewhat messy.

This book is investigatory in nature. It is certainly not presented as a curriculum text in the encyclopedic sense of the term. There are many such texts already available and there will be many more to come, one imagines. *Exemplars* is intended for educators who wish to thoughtfully consider a range of viable alternatives beyond the textbook-driven curricular default so readily observable in American schools. The models and exemplars are not simple. They are in fact difficult to implement if for no other reason than to use any of them well requires a good deal of teacher and student initiative. Most things worth doing well are difficult, and I have confidence enough in our teaching profession to believe that there are many who will welcome the challenge.

For those readers who wish to probe more deeply, I have included an extensive bibliography at the back of the book.

A Further Word About the Exemplars

You will find various exemplars of curriculum throughout the book. I have separated them from the text itself, although you will find each exemplar in close proximity to the model of curriculum that it best exemplifies. For example, the Unified Science and Mathematics for Elementary Schools (USMES) curriculum is placed near the chapter on the Society-Centered Curriculum, Mortimer Adler's Paideia Proposal is placed in close proximity to the Knowledge-Centered Curriculum chapter, and so on. In addition, the exemplars are identified by margin tabs as a further means of distinguishing them from the text chapters. One could argue that theory (text chapters) and practice (exemplars) ought to be integrated as parts of a seamless whole. There may be something to that argument. However, I finally decided that it is best to consider the theoretical dimensions as entities unto themselves, especially since no particular exemplar is completely representative of any given theory, nor should it be given the realities of practice. The reader will no doubt see the relationship between theory and practice when examining each exemplar, but will at the same time perceive that theory is neat and practice is messy. As Plato noted centuries ago, the real can approximate the ideal, but it is never the same thing. So, the exemplars are what one might consider to be "reasonable instances." Why these exemplars? Why not certain others? The answer I will give to such reasonable questions is that I believe the examples I have selected are valid representations of learner-centered, society-centered, and knowledge-centered curriculums, and that they are accessible in one form or another to the reader. Some are accessible in published, commercial form. Others are accessible because they require little in the way of published materials and are more dependent on teacher's and student's will to try them than anything else. No doubt there are other examples that could also meet these qualifications, but issues of space and diminishing rates of return preclude the inclusion of a more spacious list.

1

Toward Definition(s)

Curriculum. pl. curricula [Latin = course, career (lit, and fig.)]. A course: specifically, a regular course of study or training, as at a school or university....1633... Munimenta University of Glasgow.

The Oxford English Dictionary

What Is Curriculum?

A middle school teacher facilitates a class discussion about good and evil as portrayed in J. R. R. Tolkien's *Lord of the Rings*. The students are encouraged to cite specific references from the book or film in order to support their arguments. They are asked to make connections to their own lives and to the society they see about them. They are challenged to find other examples in literature as a homework assignment and for grist for further discussion... .

A child brings a grasshopper in a jar to school and asks the teacher why it isn't green like it is in the pictures she has seen. The child has already named her grasshopper, "Hoppy." The teacher asks the child if she would like to learn more about grasshoppers. The child is excited and says, "yes," she would. A study of insects has begun, and the child has participated as an author of the curriculum... .

Students studying ecosystems in a high school biology class are challenged by their teacher to become involved in the restoration of a stream where salmon once migrated and spawned. The class works cooperatively with the local parks department. Students find themselves volunteering their after school and week-end time to make the project a success... .

Each of these scenarios has several things in common. Teachers are challenging students to think and to act. Each scenario has content of one kind or another: A course of study is evident in each case. Learning is taking place. Students are actively involved, although their involvement is rather different in each situation. These are mere glimpses, to be sure. What might happen next is unknown to the reader. We can guess at the possibilities.

Of Origins and Metaphors

The term *curriculum* is of Latin origin, and it comes to us through the Old French verb, *currere*, meaning "to run." Related terms include current, currency, and courier. Translated into English, curriculum means, roughly, a course, as in a running course. Over time and for school purposes, it has come to signify a course of study. As you can see from the excerpt in the unabridged *Oxford English Dictionary*, its first known applications in English were in documents of Scottish higher education, with particular reference to its usage at the University of Glasgow in the 17th Century.

The word *curriculum* is a metaphor that takes figurative meaning from literal meaning. Thus a running course becomes a course of study. There is nothing unusual about that. Consider, for example, the term *kindergarten* (children's garden). Now it is certainly the case that kindergarten, a product of the Romantic Movement, is a more beautiful metaphor than curriculum. The imaginative idea of a children's garden evokes compelling imagery, so powerful that it has protected the kindergarten over the years against the on-slaughts of those who would make of it a junior first grade. It is also true that kindergarten is a less clumsy term for English speakers than is curriculum, a noun of the neuter gender set in the nominative case, pretty tough sledding for people who basically ignore case and gender in their spoken and written language.

How do you describe more than one curriculum? Well, the Latin plural form is "curricula," but just as often we tend to Anglicize it into "curriculums." All this is vexatious to say the least. As Oliva (1982, p. 5) laconically noted, "The amorphous nature of the word curriculum has given rise over the years to many interpretations." Indeed, there are many definitions and points of view, as we shall see. So many definitions and descriptions have been offered up in recent years that the poor old word can mean just about anything your want it to mean.

Curriculum as Prescription

Attempts to define curriculum tend to be prescriptive, descriptive, or some combination of the two. Prescriptive definitions provide us with what "ought" to happen, and they more often than not take the form of a plan, an intended program, or some kind of expert opinion about what needs to take place in the course of study. In that sense, they have a future orientation, a sense of things to come. Of course, in the case of medical prescriptions, the majority are apparently never filled, and of those prescriptions that patients bother to have filled by the pharmacists, it is not known how many are actually followed accurately. The best guess is that most are not. There is some parallel to this in the world of the school curriculum since the teacher, like the patient, will ultimately decide whether the prescription will be followed. The developer proposes, but the teacher disposes.

Here are several *prescriptive* definitions of curriculum:

> A prescribed body of knowledge and methods by which it might be communicated. *Alan Block (1998)*

> …the master plan, devised by educators and other adults in a community, state, or nation that will best serve their needs, and, as they see it, the needs of their children. *Donald Cay (1966)*

> A plan or program for all the experiences that the learner encounters under the direction of the school. *Peter Oliva (1997)*

> A plan for learning. *Hilda Taba (1962)*

That series of experiences that children and youth must do and experience by way of developing abilities to do the things well that make up the affairs of adult life; and to be in all respects what adults should be. *Franklin Bobbitt (1918)*

So, we are told in the preceding definitions that the curriculum is basically a plan, a map, a prescription to be followed. It is a pre-existent artifact, pre-existent in the sense that it is completed, ready to go, and all that is lacking is implementation. We can find such curriculums in state or district curriculum guides, in textbooks and related materials adopted for school use in various subject areas, and in the daily lesson plans of teachers.

Curriculum as Experience

There probably is no such thing as an estimable set of plans apart from the way things really are. This thought has led a number of people to think about the curriculum, not merely in terms of how things ought to be according to expert advice, but how things are in real classrooms. Descriptive definitions, therefore, attempt to inform us of what happens when the planned curriculum is engaged, They provide "glimpses" of the curriculum in action, although those glimpses are only occasionally based on systematic observation and empirical evidence from classrooms. Rather they tend to be descriptive in the sense that whatever one might happen to see occurring in classrooms is in fact the curriculum. The key term in descriptive definitions is "experience," so we might also call this the experienced curriculum.

Here are several examples of *descriptive* definitions of curriculum:

All the experiences children have under the guidance of teachers. *Hollis Caswell and Doak Campbell (1935)*

The set of actual experiences and perceptions of the experiences that each individual learner has of his or her program of education. *Glen Hass (1987)*

Those learnings each child selects, accepts, and incorporates into himself to act with, on, and upon, in subsequent experiences. *Thomas Hopkins (1941)*

All experiences of the child for which the school accepts responsibility. *W. B. Ragan (1960)*

The reconstruction of knowledge and experience that enables the learner to grow in exercising intelligent control of subsequent knowledge and experience. *Daniel Tanner and Laurel Tanner (1995)*

As you can see, these definitions are certainly different from the first set. For starters, they tend to be retrospective rather than predictive. Experience implies the idea that something has happened. If I asked you the difference between planning a vacation and experiencing a vacation, I am sure you would have little trouble providing a number of insights. If I asked you to talk about the difference between preparing for a job and actually working at that job, again, I can only imagine you could speak authoritatively to the matter. Addressing the matter of happiness in life, Aristotle wrote that only in looking back on life experiences are we qualified to judge whether we had found it.

This is not to say that one must choose between curriculum as plan or experience. There have been many attempts over the years to define curriculum both prescriptively and descriptively. Such definitions tend to imply *authority* (the school) and hence some kind of plan while also taking into account what happens when the plan is implemented. Here are a couple of them:

> An interrelated set of plans and experiences which a student completes under the guidance of the school. *C. Marsh and K. Stafford (1984)*

> The formal and informal content and process by which learners gain knowledge and understanding, develop skills, and alter attitudes, appreciations, and values under the auspices of the that school. *Ronald Doll (1996)*

And finally, curriculum definitions range from the terse and austere to the jargonesque and agglomerate. If one of the two following definitions says too little to be helpful and the other appears to have been written by a committee. Well, caveat lector (let the reader beware). Here they are; I will leave it to you to decide which is which:

> The deliberate arrangement of subject matter. *Arthur Foshay (1968)*

> We find curriculum still being construed very much in terms of 'packages' of skills and content at a time when a metaphor like 'platforms' seems much more apposite.... The postmodern philosophical concepts of anti-foundationalism and post-epistemological standpoint invoke logics and sensibilities that privilege active pursuit of ways of looking at the world rather than absorbing predefined content and skills grounded in extant worldviews. The learner who masters 'platforms' can proactively generate interpretations and frame designs that in turn generate their own learning and innovation agendas and,

ultimately, worldviews. *A. de Alba, E. Gonzalez-Gaudino, C. Lankshear, M. Peters (2000)*

Have you found a favorite so far? Perhaps you'd like to write your own tentative definition of curriculum at this point. Go ahead, give it a try.

Summing Up

I'll close this brief introductory chapter by offering two more definitions, one rather narrow and strict constructivist, the other rather all encompassing and open to interpretation. Here is Arthur Bestor's (1955) description of the curriculum as limited to academic subjects:

> "Curriculum must consist essentially of disciplined study in five great areas: (i) command of the mother tongue and the systematic study of grammar, literature, and writing; (ii) mathematics; (iii) sciences; (iv) history; (v) foreign language." *Arthur Bestor (1955)*

Bestor's perspective is limited not merely to school subjects but to certain school subjects. He excludes the arts, physical education, "life skills" courses (driver education, word processing, etc.), school-to-work experiences, and a number of other curricular offerings typically found in schools today. In that sense he takes what we could safely call a narrow, strict constructionist approach to the curriculum, only the basics. But what are the basics? In ancient Greece, physical education and the arts were thought to be basic. Aristotle himself went so far as to claim that physical education is more crucial in the bringing up of the young than is academic education. He ranked moral education as a priority in the middle of those two.

Contrast Bestor's restrictive description with the wide open meaning offered by Gay (1990):

> The entire culture of the school—not just subject matter content. *Gay (1990)*

Apparently Gay disagrees with Bestor, bestowing on the term enough latitude to cover everything including, one imagines, the kitchen sink, connected to the school experience. The "entire culture of the school" would certainly include the lunchroom, brief conversations held at lockers during change of classes, after school sports and drama, the bus ride to and from school, the teachers' union, even the clothing the students, teachers, and others wear to school. Nothing gets left out.

Where does this leave us? I think we must find shelter under the umbrella of adjectives. Modifiers come to our rescue. Taking an adjectival perspective allows us the luxury of describing the curriculum as planned, written, enacted, measured, experienced, learned, collateral, incidental, concomitant, implicit, hidden, null, and extra, to name a few. We can describe the curriculum as technical, practical, and reflective. We can think of the curriculum by employing such philosophical descriptors as essentialist, perennialist, progressive, and reconstructionist. We can advance the process one step further by offering hyphenated modifiers such as child-centered, society-centered, knowledge-centered, and teacher-centered. Each of these modifiers offers a specific perspective on the multifaceted nature of curriculum. All this is more than word play, to be sure. But these are matters to take up in chapters yet to come.

Your Turn

- ◆ What are your common-sense thoughts on these three *centers*?
  - Learner-centered
  - Society-centered
  - Knowledge-centered
- ◆ What would you like to know about how each one is conceptualized by the models we will be examining?

2

Reading
Between the Lines

Train up a child in the way he should go,
and when he is old he will not turn from it.

Proverbs 22:6

One of the most far reaching changes of thought
in human history is the modern view of the freedom
of children as the basis of education.

A. S. Neill

Planned vs. Experienced Curriculum

As you read Chapter One, you saw that some educators prefer to think about the curriculum in terms of what should happen, that is, a plan. Others prefer to think of it in terms of what actually happens, the experience. Take your choice: curriculum as prescription or curriculum as description. Another way to consider the matter is in terms of intentions versus outcomes. However, the use of the term "outcomes," especially with reference to outcomes-based education in recent years, has muddied the waters. If we think of outcomes in terms of what actually occurs, then we use the term in the experiential sense. On the other hand, if we mean a forecast of skills and knowledge to be mastered, then we are in fact using it from the point of view of the planned curriculum.

You may be thinking that the curriculum can be both planned and experienced. This is true, to be sure, but certain questions inevitably arise to complicate the picture. For example, who should do the planning: curriculum developers? state department personnel? teachers? students? textbook publishers? The essence of this question is whether outside experts or those who live with the curriculum are best suited to do the planning. And, if we wish to consider the experienced curriculum, who will provide the descriptions of what happens: teachers? students? trained observers? I'm sure you are familiar with eyewitness accounts of a particular event that leave you wondering whether the eyewitnesses actually saw the same event, so different are their accounts. Imagine accounting accurately, faithfully, for the experience in a place as complex as a school classroom. It's not an easy thing.

Narrow vs. Expansive Definitions

The other obvious difference of opinion that surfaces in Chapter One is the "strict constructionist" versus "life experience" argument. Strict constructionists define the curriculum as the course of study. Typically this means the separate school subjects are delivered in the form of some scope and sequence. Life experientialists define the curriculum in a more all-encompassing fashion, particularly taking into account the feelings, perceptions, and attitudes of individuals and groups that develop over time. In one sense, this difference suggests the idea of curriculum as an object that exists independent of experience versus the idea of curriculum as the subjective experience of individuals and groups. The first definition implies that the same curriculum can be taught many times and many places, for example, geography or fractions or American literature. The second definition implies that any curriculum is situated and idiosyncratic and that there is no such thing as the curriculum apart from how it is experienced in a particular setting. Anyone who has taught two or more sections or classes of the "same" subject will tell you that you have the subject matter and you have the experience.

The arguments presented above are arguments of long standing. The best each of us can do is to settle them on the basis of reflection and assessment, individually and collegially. Good teachers have and will continue to be found in each camp. Given a choice, most teachers seem to prefer to think of themselves as embracing both.

Training Up and Leading Forth

Whatever the curriculum, however it is conceived, there remains the practical business of the day-to-day routine. Teachers are doers; they spend much of their day nurturing, encouraging, and responding to others. Much is asked of teachers, and much is given by them. It is a rare thing to encounter a teacher who thinks of his/her work as just another job. Teachers at all levels must discharge the twin duties of "training up" (from the Latin word, *educare*) and "leading forth" (from the Latin word, *educere*). These two Latin words, so close in spelling and so different in meaning, are the basis of the educational experience. Whatever the subject, separate or integrated, a teacher is shaping and setting free his/her young charges. Good teaching involves both.

Any curriculum is taught with more than one motive. For example, the teacher teaching young children to read is also teaching them to behave, to follow instructions, to consider others, to respect property, to exercise self-discipline, and to want to read for study and pleasure. We can see in these curricular purposes the business of "training up," that is, using the curriculum to develop a civil society within the classroom. And we can also imagine the teacher "leading forth" a group of children who will in time, discover for themselves the adventure of reading as a lifelong pursuit that brings its own rewards, and who will as well become deeper thinkers, more reflective persons, and better human beings as a result of reading worthwhile literature.

The curricular aspects of training up are adult directed and dedicated to shaping young lives. A curriculum must be managed somehow. The experiences students have under the guidance of mature professionals are ideally designed not merely to improve academic knowledge and skills, but to make them better citizens, people who are more aware of others and the need to practice self-control in life. This is in its most basic sense a curriculum of restraint and responsibility. These aspects of school life are praised by those who see in it a benign effect and condemned by those who see the school experience as a place where students learn to be compliant, obedient, and basically trained to preserve the status quo.

The curriculum of leading forth is adult facilitated but not adult directed. Its intent is to give students freedom and glimpses of the possible. To the extent that the school experience enables students to dream of what they might become, of how they might contribute, of why they are needed in life, to that extent it is successful. The curriculum of leading forth is a curriculum of risk taking, of intellectual and moral challenge, of freedom and opportunity. We see images of this curriculum in the student who decides that she wants to be a scientist because of the influence of her physics teacher, or in the young person who discovers the artist in himself because of a teacher's support and encouragement. And we see images of the curriculum of leading forth in the experience of young people who become involved in team building and community projects, young people who learn about citizenship, not vicariously, but first hand.

Summing Up

A purposeful school curriculum must be built on a foundation of freedom and opportunity on the one hand, and responsibility and restraint on the other. These dual functions may seem at first glance to be antithetical and contradictory. Actually, they are complementary, opposite sides of the same coin. I suggest to you that a curriculum cannot achieve its potential without such an appropriate balance. Social science systems theory informs us that a complex system (for example, a classroom or a school) functions best when it is anchored firmly at its base and is open at its top. The secure base provides students with the predictability, stability, and consistency so crucial to leading an ordered life, while the openness in the system allows for diversity, individual differences, creative efforts, risk taking, and opportunities in self-realization. This is the secret to synchronizing the complementary goals of freedom/opportunity and responsibility/restraint; a secure but open system.

A curriculum needs to be built with this in mind. At the base are several assumptions and rules, for example, this is a class where it is expected that students will study the material faithfully, bring a participatory attitude toward discussions and activities, treat others with respect, exercise self-discipline, and follow a few simple rules. At the top there exists an openness that encourages initiative, exploration, individual and team efforts, creativity, differing interests, and multiple ways to learn. This leaves us with a curriculum that accommodates the narrow function (course of study) as well as the broad function (school experience); a curriculum that includes both preplanning by teachers and other professionals as well as student involvement in shaping the experience.

Your Turn

Before we consider a few key questions regarding any curriculum model, take the time to consider your own.

- What are your thoughts on the two functions?
- Take a moment to write down what you think each should (and should not) include based on your experience and ideas so far.
  - Course of study
  - School experience

3

A Few Questions...

It is better to know some of the questions than all of the answers.

James Thurber

Near the beginning it is useful to approach the curriculum from a perspective of questions. The questions ought to be about what really matters. The questions should provide a kind of structure or essence of what we believe about education. The point is not that we will reach common answers, not that we will agree on all the details, and not that we will find the Holy Grail of the curriculum. Rather, the point is that we will have at least asked the same important questions. The purpose of this chapter is to raise the key questions about the nature of the curriculum, who it involves and how. Why we approach it the way we do, its sense of purpose, and finally, what we hope to achieve through it.

What are the goals of the curriculum?

We keep students in school for hours on end, day after day, year after year. School ranks second only to television viewing in terms of the time children and adolescents spend with it. School is required, and television viewing is largely voluntary. The fact that we require it means that we must think the school experience is valuable, probably in a number of ways. This raises several basic questions. What are we trying accomplish? What things can be done better through the school experience than anywhere else? How should life in school change a person? What is the profile of the successful school graduate? These questions address the goal structure of school and the curriculum.

It is typical to think of the school and the curriculum as the center-piece of schooling as advancing four major goals. The goals represent our shared vision of results of schooling. Those goals are

- ◆ academic knowledge,
- ◆ participatory citizenship,
- ◆ self-realization, and
- ◆ career opportunity.

Should all subjects of the curriculum be held responsible for advancing all four goals? Can certain subjects contribute more than others to certain of the goals? Should each of the goals be given equal weight? Are four goals too many? Do you even agree that these ought to be the goals we ascribe to? What other goals are left out if we limit ourselves to these four?

The goal structure is significant because if we take it seriously it sets the foundation for what happens day to day. Goals represent long-term strategic thinking about what is important. This is why they should be clear and few in number. Laundry lists of goals tend to be ignored. Unclear goals typically go unrealized. The question sometimes arises whether goals and objectives are the same thing. I think not. Goals represent strategy. Objectives represent tactics, or how we achieve a strategy on a day-to-day basis. The relationship between goals and objectives is necessarily symbiotic. They depend on each other, but goals are more fundamental because they set the course while objectives help us stay the course.

What knowledge is of most worth?

This difficult question was posed in essay form in the middle of the 19th Century by the English philosopher, Herbert Spencer. Spencer saw about him a changing world. The most dramatic and obvious effects of change were those brought about by the Industrial Revolution, to be sure, but there were others as well, including investigations into the origins and evolution of species and a host of discoveries in pure and applied science. If the world was no longer to be considered an unchanging, static place, then what were the implications of change for the school curriculum? Of course, if Spencer were alive today he would be even more impressed by the accelerating rate of change in the order of things. His monumental essay, titled, "What Knowledge Is of Most Worth?" was published in 1859, the same year in which Charles Darwin published his book, *On the Origin of Species*. It was, curiously, the very year in which John Dewey, considered to be the foremost philosopher of education in American history, was born, and in which Horace Mann, often called the father of the American public school movement, died.

The curricular question of what to leave in and what to leave out is particularly difficult, far more difficult a question than it was in Spencer's time. The biology curriculum, for example, changes daily if were take into account the rapid developments in genetic research alone. New chapters are added to the history and geography texts as maps are redrawn and political systems rise and fall. More novels, short stories, plays, and poems are being written and published today than ever before, and they compete for inclusion with those already present in the literary canon. It is said that mathematics is advancing at such a rapid rate that even most mathematicians have difficulty understanding the articles written in advanced journals of mathematics.

So, if we were to reinvent the curriculum, to start over, to decide anew what knowledge should be taught at school, what should we decide? Would we keep all the old subjects in place? Would we keep them in place but radically redefine them? Would we drop certain subjects from the curriculum with the idea that their time has come and gone? What new subjects might be added? Should students study philosophy? game theory? religion? architecture? A good example of a school subject that has yet to be widely accepted is earth and space science. One reason often given for this is historical. Simply said, the biology, chemistry, physics sequence got there first, and there was no room left for it in the secondary curriculum. Should it take its place alongside biology, chemistry, and physics? Beyond such questions, should the school curriculum be approached on some basis other than separate subjects?

Guessing the Future

As you think about what knowledge is of most worth, you need to do so from a perspective of educated guesswork or probabilities about the future. What knowledge will students need as the 21st Century continues to unfold? Students entering school today will retire from their careers during those years closer to the 22nd Century than to the 20th. How can we even presume to know what knowledge they will need? This has always been a challenge for educators, but the challenge is heightened today because of what Spencer saw more than a century and a half ago, that is, the rapidly accelerating rate of change.

What values should be taught and learned?

One answer to this question is that the most important values are timeless. They include honesty, integrity, justice, courage, duty, compassion, etc. But even if we were to agree on a set of estimable values, could we agree on how to teach them and how they ought to be learned? Just as knowledge is more than product, so are values. The process of how we acquire knowledge and values is equally important.

Values are often taught and learned along the way, through what is sometimes called the hidden curriculum or the concomitant curriculum. Given this thought, what teacher behaviors and student behaviors ought to be expected? To what extent do the values transacted in classrooms represent anything more than cultural norms that are not so much right or wrong, but just the way "we" do things? For example, a teacher might expect a student to look him/her in the eye when responding to a direct question, but there is no empirical evidence that looking someone in the eye is related to honesty, integrity, etc., except perhaps that it is expected in certain culture groups.

Values of voice, power, authority, collegiality, self-realization, and freedom of movement are hardly trivial matters. But how often do they come up as issues in curriculum development? To what extent are these values age-related or developmentally-related? The more we consider the question of what values are to be taught and learned, the more we see that there are the obvious matters and there are subtle matters, many of which are never really examined. Some years ago, the curriculum researcher John Goodlad (1984) pointed out that teachers out-talk students by a ratio of about 3:1. This represents a value. Is it a good value? Should it change? Teachers are typically outnumbered about 25:1 by students, so Goodlad's figure doesn't really give much talking time to students. Yet we know that intelligence and speech co-develop, and that human beings need to talk, to express themselves. Still, some teachers think that this is something that can wait 'til after school.

Finally, to what extent ought cultural sensitivity come into play in attempting to answer the question of appropriate values? To the extent that our schools have become more responsive to diversity in the population and to changing societal norms, we see behaviors and expectations in a state of flux. For some, these changes represent a decline in standards, while for others many were long over due.

What essential skills are at stake?

A curriculum is based on knowledge and values, but it must also be based on skills. Skills are about know-how. Skills found in the curriculum range from how to use a pair of scissors to cut along a line to how to present your ideas in a tactful and persuasive manner. Skills include knowing to invert the divisor and multiply as well as having the ability to discern form, texture, line, and perspective in a painting. There are intellectual skills, social skills, physical skills, and emotional skills. Can or should the schools attempt to teach them all?

- What skills are particularly relevant in the context of certain subject matter?
- Are there skills that cut across the curriculum?
- What skills are best taught directly? through modeling?
- To what extent are skills developmental, age- related?
- What happens when a curriculum becomes little more than a set of skills to be learned?
- At what point does an inordinate emphasis on skills in the curriculum reduce education to training?

What is an appropriate view of society?

This may not seem, initially at least, to be a question about curriculum. But after all, school is an agent of society, a subset of the larger society, so finally we must consider the kind of society we want to prepare students for. John Dewey was quite clear in his opinion that a school is in fact a miniature society and that it ought to take democratic forms. Why? Because that is the kind of society he favored, and he argued that school is not preparation for life, but that school is life itself.

My observations of school in the former USSR and in present-day Russia have led me to believe that Dewey's idea of society was very different from theirs. I have seen very little there to convince me that what Russians have wanted and presently want of their schools is that they become miniature democracies. So, what kind of society do we want? And to what extent can practicing that society at school make that society become a reality? In other words, does the school curriculum have the power to shape students' ideas of what an appropriate society should be like? Will students replicate their school experience in the larger society?

Beyond the questions of the political/social organization of society, what must schools do to help students to succeed in life? If a society values literacy, numeracy, historical, and scientific knowledge, then what are the implications for the curriculum? If a society values the pursuit of happiness, personal liberty, and genuine community, what does this mean for the curriculum?

What do we believe about students?

Do we believe that students actually want to learn? Do we believe that they are naturally curious explorers? Do we believe they need to work together? Do we believe that each student is different? Do we believe that all students can succeed? And if so, what exactly do we mean by that? Do we believe that students should mainly receive knowledge at school? Or do we believe that they ought to discover and construct knowledge for themselves?

Bernard Weiner's (1995) attribution theory suggests that we inevitably attribute certain motivations to the behaviors of others. In doing so, we form beliefs, rightly or not, about why people act in certain ways. In a classroom, a teacher holds certain perceptions about why students act the way they do. In turn, students hold perceptions of those around them. Consider the following statement by the historian Francis Fukuyama (1995, p. 31). As you read his words, substitute the terms "classroom" and "school" for "society" and "teachers and students" for "workers."

> "A high-trust society can organize its workplace on a more flexible and group-oriented basis, with more responsibility delegated to lower levels of the organization. Low-trust societies, by contrast, must fence in and isolate their workers with a series of bureaucratic rules."
>
> *Francis Fukuyama*

What is a high-trust curriculum? What would it look like? How would it be different from business as usual? Thoughtful teachers cannot escape the reality of knowing that their perceptions of the students they teach are as much the basis of the curriculum, perhaps more, than the subject matter itself.

What are the implications for a pluralistic society?

We've raised some questions about individuals and society, but those were designed to get you thinking in a general sense about what is appropriate. Take a moment to consider this: the 1940 United States census informed us that three adults lived in the typical American home. Further, that census revealed that at least one, and often two, of those adults worked or stayed at home. The 2000 census revealed a different America in which fewer than two adults are found in the typical home, with a fairly high probability that no adult is home to greet children after school. Imagine the implications of this change for differences in childhood and adolescent supervision and support.

Consider for a moment the changes in the ethnic composition of American society within the last generation (see Fig. 3.1). Our country has continued to be enriched over the years by waves of immigration, resulting in a highly diverse society. Additionally, certain societal groups, some of long standing, that were previously excluded from the privileges of a meaningful education are now participating more fully. African Americans, for example, began arriving in Colonial America in 1619, a year before the Pilgrims established their colony at Plymouth.

No curriculum can exist apart from those who participate in it. American education is changing, and it must continue to change if it is to meet the needs of the young in a pluralistic society. Fair and equal treatment of all individuals and groups remains a goal, one that is far from being achieved. The question of the implications of all this for the curriculum looms large.

**Figure 3.1. Racial and Ethnic Composition
of the United States, 1999 and 2025**

Ethnic Group	1999	2025	% Change
White	71.9%	62.0%	- 10.1%
Black	12.1%	12.9%	+ 0.8%
Hispanic	11.5%	18.2%	+ 6.7%
Asian & Other	4.5%	7.0%	+ 2.5%

Source: Population Reference Bureau in partnership with demographer Bill Frey et al. at the University of Michigan's Social Science Data Analysis Network, available June 10, 2003 at www.prb.org .

Summing Up

The questions raised in this chapter are designed to encourage a curriculum conversation, one that seeks understanding rather than final answers. The conversation needs to be ongoing and open-ended. Any faculty that is serious about curriculum improvement needs to reflect on such matters as: "what do we believe about students?" and "what do we believe about knowledge?" Further, students themselves must be challenged to think about and express their ideas on these crucial questions.

School life has about it a sense of immediacy. Teachers and students rarely seem to have time to reflect on why they do what they do. Rather, most of the day is spent responding and reacting to situations. Raising and attempting to answer questions of purpose is hardly a luxury if we really want to make the curriculum experience more meaningful, useful, and truthful. The teachers and students who do accept the necessity of such reflective questioning and assessment will have crossed a frontier from school as merely a place of teaching to school as a place of learning.

Your Turn

By now you have recognized that the 'Your Turn' closure to each chapter is a reflective process. Apart from asking you to think of the concrete examples of your experience, and to identify how they fit into these curriculum models, we should also ask you to consider your own sense of purpose. As mentioned above, this is usually regarded as a luxury in the press of meeting the challenges and demands of the school day.

So treat yourself to the most basic of reflective questions before you continue your tour of curriculum.

- ◆ Why are there schools?
- ◆ Why are you an educator?
- ◆ Are these exercises at the end of the chapters easy or hard for you to take time for?

This account of the central character in John Knowles' book, *Peace Breaks Out* (1981), is a scene from the story of life at Devon School in the years following World War II. Pete Hallam, a decorated war hero who has accepted a teaching position at his old school, faces his very first day of classes, an experience most teachers well remember.

Two days later, on the opening day of classes, Pete met with his twelve students in American History. Even though he was underqualified for a teacher at Devon, holding only a B.A. in the subject, and was aware than an exception had been made for him in this appointment, he felt equal to dealing with the situation.

For one thing, the physical arrangements for meeting classes at Devon were congenial to him. Teacher and students sat around an oval table and together dealt with [the] subject. He did not have to act like Moses handing down the law from Mount Sinai to them. They were meeting, almost, conferring together and on the same level. He thought back to one or two grossly inadequate teachers he had himself had in college, lecturers who from the remoteness of their position on the podium got away, academically speaking, with murder, droning pedantic bores who failed completely to reach their isolated and helpless students. He was resolved that, whatever else might happen, he was not going to be that kind of teacher. In this sunny classroom in Stephens Hall, in wooden armchairs around this mahogany table, they would deal with American History and, he was confident, something would get learned.

John Knowles (1981)

4

The
Progressive Paradigm

There is, I think, no point in the philosophy of progressive education which is sounder than its emphasis upon the importance of the participation of the learner in the formation of purposes which direct his activities in the learning process, just as there is no defect in traditional education greater than its failure to secure the active co-operation of the pupil in construction of the purposes involved in his studying.

John Dewey

A Brief History

The progressive paradigm, often used as a point of contrast to signify the "new" curriculum versus the essentialist or "old" curriculum, has in fact been around in one form or another for centuries. When the Roman educator, Quintilian, proclaimed "the Doctrine of Interest" in the 1st Century A.D., his point was that the curriculum is best determined by the interest of the learner, an idea that centuries later became a cornerstone of progressive educational thought. Quintilian wrote that students should study what they want to study because subject matter forced upon the learner has little positive lasting effect and considerable lasting negative effect. He also concluded that corporal punishment hardened the heart of the child and that it was pedagogically unsound. This idea, too, would in time take its place in the progressive worldview.

In the 18th and 19th Centuries, such luminaries as Jean-Jacques Rousseau, Johann Pestalozzi, and Friedrich Froebel sang the praises of Romanticism as it related to child-centered learning. Rousseau's classic work, *Emile*, was a work of fiction describing the "natural" education of a young boy whose tutor emphasized experiential and relational learning over bookish studies. Rousseau, who even by today's standards would be considered radical, criticized bookish learning as inappropriate to the development (moral and intellectual) of young minds.

The Swiss educator Pestalozzi is considered the father of modern elementary education with his emphasis on the creation of a nurturing environment, attention to individual growth and development, and learning through concrete experience. Pestalozzi's insistence on love and kindness as first principles of education drew many admirers, even though in fact the schools of his day mainly continued to be places of coercion, restraint, and physical and mental hardship. Still, his ideas had staying power, and they are taken for granted by progressives today.

Froebel, the German educator credited with the founding of the kindergarten or "children's garden," reinvented early childhood education with his insistence on the importance of play, physical activity, creativity, and spiritual development. Froebel was a prototypical Romantic with his notions of childhood as a time of innocence, wonder, and hope. His emphasis on nature and the spiritual unity of the universe proved to be appealing educational ideas to many who were interested in true educational reform. His Child Nurture and Activity Institute, which he in time, beautifully renamed the Kindergarten, became a model of early childhood education that spread throughout Europe and America in the 19th and 20th Centuries.

In America, the progressive movement was certainly based on the work of these European thinkers, but it took on its own peculiar trappings. The movement gathered momentum in the late 19th Century and continued apace into the 20th. Its roots can clearly be traced to Romanticism, but it came to represent more than that. It evolved over time, variously taking on elements of romanticism, behaviorism, pragmatism, and social activism. Needless to say, progressive education has come to mean different things to different people, and it is not easy to categorize.

John Dewey's work at the University of Chicago Laboratory School from 1894 to 1904 gave national visibility to his ideas of education for democracy, community involvement in learning, student empowerment, and applied problem solving. Dewey was convinced that the social aspects of public education are more purposeful than even the academic aspects. He came to view the study of academic subject matter as an end in itself as misguided. His philosophy of instrumentalism, as he labeled it, called for the direct application of knowledge and skills toward the solution of real problems. The Unified Science and Mathematics for Elementary Schools (USMES) curriculum, described later in this book, was begun as an attempt to resurrect Dewey's ideas of real-world problem solving based on the needs and interests of students. Legend has it that one of Dewey's first acts as director of the laboratory school was to search out and purchase tables in a Chicago warehouse because classrooms with rows of desks were antithetical to the socializing experiences so necessary to school life. A graduate student of mine teaching mathematics in a Tacoma, Washington, middle school was so impressed with this historical anecdote that he followed suit. When I asked him if it made a difference in teaching and learning, he replied that it was the single best decision he ever made about classroom life.

Dewey argued persuasively that education at its best is based on the continuous reconstruction of experiences emanating from student interest and active investigation. Dewey, however, was less a romantic than he was a pragmatist, interested in "what works," especially in terms of building a democratic society. The idea that the school experience ought to more accurately reflect "real life" became a central tenet of progressivism and a uniquely American contribution to the movement. Such thinking leads quite naturally to an emphasis on community involvement, life skills in the curriculum, applied courses in agriculture (Future Farmers of America) and homemaking (Future Homemakers of America), group and schoolwide projects, and the idea of integrated "units" of study as opposed to an "inert," separate-disciplines, textbook-dominated curriculum.

In addition to Dewey's work at his Laboratory School at the University of Chicago, great progressive experiments were carried out in Gary, Indiana; Dalton, Massachusetts; Winnetka, Illinois; and at Teachers College of Columbia University. The common threads included emphases on learner interest and initiative, project learning, integrated studies, life experience, social adjustment, extracurricular activity, and core curriculum. Prominent leaders of the movement included Colonel Francis Parker, William Kilpatrick, Harold Rugg, and George Counts, to name a few.

Francis Parker had journeyed to Germany in the 1870s where he studied progressive educational theory, particularly the work of the psychologist and philosopher, Johann Herbart (1776–1841), who had stressed the importance of relating new ideas and skills to the child's own experience. Parker returned to the United States and implemented a number of innovative ideas in the Quincy, Massachusetts' schools, particularly the Herbartian ideas of experiential learning, informal instruction, and kinder, gentler discipline. Parker served as principal of the Cook County Normal School from 1883 to 1899, and founded the Chicago Institute in 1899. The institute in time, became a part of the School of Education at the University of Chicago. Parker's influence on John Dewey was considerable to say the least.

Kilpatrick, a disciple of Dewey's at Columbia University (although Dewey came in time to disagree with many of Kilpatrick's ideas), wrote an article in 1918 in the *Teachers College Record*, titled, "The Project Method." Few journal articles in the field of education have so electrified America's teachers, with something like 100,000 requests for reprints. Kilpatrick's idea of purposeful, active project learning, especially contrasted to a curriculum of textbooks and separate subjects, quickly became a cornerstone of progressive educational practice.

Harold Rugg and George Counts were instrumental in developing and alternative form of the progressive movement, away from its more child-centered preoccupations, creating a reconstructionist, social activist agenda. Counts' book, *Dare the Schools Build a New Social Order?* (1932), was a clarion call to educators to change the world. Only the young are capable of making a better world, the thinking went, and teachers need to mobilize them, take advantage of the idealism, and make the school experience relevant to the society at large. These were days in which capitalism as an economic order was seriously being questioned, especially given the hard times of the Great Depression, and the capitalist system's seeming inability to restore prosperity. Many intellectuals, including Dewey and others, embraced socialism and flirted with communism as answers to society's problems. World War II put such thinking on the shelf, and communism has not since recovered its influence as a serious theme in American education. Today the society-centered, reconstructionist idea remains as a minor but appealing theme to those educators who see their task as changing the world.

In 1918, the National Education Association (NEA) published the report of the Commission on Reorganization of Secondary Education, listing the "Seven Cardinal Principles of Secondary Education" (see Fig. 4.2).

Figure 4.1. The Seven Cardinal Principles of Secondary Education, Commission on Reorganization of Secondary Education (1918)

> *The 7 Cardinal Principles of Secondary Education*
>
> Health
>
> Command of fundamental processes
>
> Worthy home membership
>
> Vocational competence
>
> Citizenship
>
> Worthy use of leisure time
>
> Ethical character

This publication sent a clear signal that the education of the young must be based on those "relevant" experiences necessary to a meaningful life rather than on bookish learning. This marked the beginning of the American comprehensive secondary school, complete with vocational as well as academic tracks, courses in life adjustment, guidance, and counseling as part of the school experience. It was also the beginning of the middle school movement, with units of study, project learning, and integrated curriculum. The middle school, as opposed to the junior high school, is a fundamental contribution of the progressive educational movement.

The Eight-Year Study

In 1932 the Progressive Education Association (PEA) commissioned what was to become known as the *Eight Year Study*. The purpose of this large-scale investigation was to determine whether students who attended progressive high schools were as well prepared academically for college and university study as were students who attended traditional high schools. The data showed that indeed they were, and further, that students from progressive schools were more involved than their traditional school counterparts in such university functions as co-curricular and extra curricular activities. However, the United States was preparing for war just as the study reached its conclusion, and little interest was shown at the time in the results. Still, the results of the Eight Year Study suggest that progressive methods are viable, and one can point to numerous lasting contributions and effects of progressive educational ideas in the school curriculum.

The period from 1918 through the 1930s was the high water mark of the progressive movement. In fact the PEA no longer exists. But progressive educational philosophy continues to play a major role in the school curriculum. Many of the effects seem permanent, and progressive influence continues today in the form of constructivism, block scheduling, elective courses, non-graded schools, authentic and performance assessment, whole language learning, and a variety of other forms.

Progressive Curriculum

A progressive curriculum emphasizes the quality of experience and processes of growth and development over content and skill mastery. This key distinction is often overlooked, and without being clear about it, you cannot build a progressive curriculum. But on what basis does one determine whether the emphasis is on the quality of the experience? The answer is found in the notion of learner needs and interest, based on intrinsic motivation to learn. When the child (or anyone for that matter) genuinely desires to learn something, lasting growth is possible. Few people would disagree with this assumption. Where the matter becomes sticky is over the contention that there are things that young people "need" to learn about which they might well be indifferent. The progressive answer to this problem is to make the curriculum, the learning experience, purposeful, appealing, and motivating.

Teacher Role

The role of the teacher is that of facilitator of learning. It is summed up by the cliché, "the guide on the side rather than the sage on the stage." The teacher guides but seldom directs. The teacher listens but seldom tells. The teacher works behind the scenes to create an environment that is appealing, inviting, and stimulating. As both John Dewey and Jean Piaget noted, teaching is the creation of an environment in which students can grow intellectually, socially, and morally. And as Piaget insisted, telling is not teaching. Such a curriculum demands variety, choices, and opportunities for learners to experiment, to take risks, to practice taking the initiative. See Figure 4.2 for a summary of key elements of progressive curricular emphasis.

Dewey argued that the best education occurs when the teacher becomes a learner and the learners become teachers. This insightful statement implies modeling on the part of the teacher and opportunity for the students to express themselves as people who have something to share with others. It opens up the possibilities for peer teaching, for cooperative efforts, and for the teacher to study and therefore become more knowledgeable about the students themselves. As Rousseau wrote in the preface to *Emile* (1762),

"...make it your first task to know your students better for you surely do not know them."

Figure 4.2. Elements of a Progressive Curriculum

Emphasis	◆ Experiential or process focus ◆ Integrated studies approach ◆ Learner interest ◆ Fluid course of study ◆ Developmentally appropriate practice ◆ Real-world emphases
Teaching	◆ Indirect instruction ◆ Teacher as facilitator ◆ Variety in teaching ◆ Peer teaching/mentoring
Learning	◆ Student initiated & directed ◆ Cooperative groups ◆ Community involvement ◆ Relational/Collaborative ◆ Inquiry/Discovery
Environment	◆ Constructivist ◆ Cross-age grouping ◆ Team teaching ◆ Fluid/Open ◆ Non-graded, continuous progress ◆ Emphasis on affect
Assessment	◆ Formative ◆ Student-initiated ◆ Authentic/performance ◆ Reflective thinking ◆ Anecdotal

Team teaching, team planning, and site-based decision making are all integral parts of teacher role in a progressive curriculum. As teachers and administrators practice collaborative efforts, they are more able to translate this experience into their teaching. A progressive curriculum is a relational curriculum, and teacher isolation, a deep and abiding problem in schools, must be transformed into teacher community.

Student Role

The center of gravity shifts to the student(s) in a progressive curriculum. This means student planning, decision making, and studying are of greatest interest. The initiative belongs to the student(s). Learning is based on interest, and it is collaborative, relational, and project oriented. Growth is considered not merely from an academic point of view but from emotional, social, and moral perspectives as well. The quality of the experience is at stake, and the student is in the best position of all to determine the level of quality. Students are expected to be active, in all that implies from physical movement to social involvement to performance to student government. Progressives use the term "community" to describe their classrooms and schools. All that community implies, that is, democracy, participation, the commonweal, citizenship, and esprit de corps are integral to the effort.

Students are expected not merely to learn academic knowledge and skills, but to use knowledge as a tool for problem solving. Problems should ideally come from real life, and students should view the disciplines of mathematics, reading, science, geography, etc., not as ends in themselves but as instruments, just as the carpenter, musician, artist, and scientist use tools to solve problems.

Environment

The progressive learning environment challenges almost every tenet of the traditional curriculum. Instead of an age-graded system, one finds cross-age grouping, continuous progress, team teaching and learning, and other fluid arrangements in which teachers and students work and play together. Team teaching and planning is often used as a means of sharing teacher strengths as well as a means of modeling cooperative work. Environments tend to be open, often in an architectural sense, but especially in the sense of freedom of movement, expression, and empowerment. Emphasis is placed on affect, and considerable effort goes into making the environment appealing, nurturing, and generally supportive of student freedom. At primary levels and occasionally into the intermediate grades, one finds interest centers, hobby corners, and space set aside as workshop. The idea that a classroom or a school should be inviting, attractive, and decorated with student work can be traced back to an early father of the progressive movement, Jon Amos Comenius, a leading educator of the 16th Century.

Assessment

The emphasis is on formative assessment, and on assessment as realized in personal growth. In a progressive curriculum, the central purpose of assessment is self-improvement or group improvement rather than external "expert" judgment and classification of learners from high to low. Assessment is generally student initiated, student monitored, and student consumed. Performance is the key because actually doing something that demands growth in skill, knowledge, and judgment is prized above paper and pencil exercises and recitation which are seen as artificial achievements of little lasting significance. Teacher reporting of growth and development (terms that progressives prefer over achievement) tend to be narrative, anecdotal, and often informal. The role of the student is paramount. The idea of student-led parent conferences, for example, is pure progressivism. Individual self-assessment and collaborative assessment are key elements of the progressive curriculum. Peer coaching and critique and group reflective assessment are also part and parcel of the progressive approach.

Summing Up

The progressive argument is basically one of freedom and opportunity. Progressives take issue with authoritarian practice, coercive learning, academic subjects taught for their own sake, and failure to take the learner's needs and interests into account. Central to the progressive vision is the idea of schools and classrooms as miniature democracies or communities in which students and teachers work together in an atmosphere of experiment and risk taking. Subject matter is viewed as a tool for problem solving and not as an end in itself. Textbooks and separate academic subjects have little place in a progressive curriculum. Students are fully expected to be involved in planning, conducting, and assessing their learning experiences.

In American education, progressivism represents a curious blend of romanticism, activism, and pragmatism, and if one looks carefully enough at its history, behaviorism. Two related but different camps of progressive education are found in the emphasis on the individual and his/her attempts at self-realization, and the emphasis on the group and its attempts to make a better world. These ideas are explored more fully in the chapters on learner-centered curriculum and society-centered curriculum.

Your Turn

◆ How do you see your own beliefs aligned with the American progressive blend of ideology?

◆ To what extent do you identify with:
  • Romanticism
  • Activism
  • Pragmatism

5

The Learner-Centered Curriculum

...if the school is to be made to fit the child rather than the other way round, the curriculum should be determined by the child's needs and interests.

John Darling

What a learner-centered perspective and model helps educators understand is that individual learners, young and old, students and teachers—like all human beings—bring with them a complex array of unique viewpoints, needs, capacities, and strengths.

Jo Sue Whisler & Barbara McCombs

The focus of this chapter is the learner-centered curriculum. This approach is sometimes known as the child-centered curriculum, but that can be a bit misleading because many of the people who are involved in learner-centered teachig and learning are not children. Another term, the student-centered curriculum, is also somewhat limiting in that it seems to separate students from teachers, who are, or also ought to be, learners themselves. The learner-centered curriculum is found in the progressive educational tradition. Clearly, its ideas and energy derive from progressive theory.

This curriculum model has been used successfully at all ages and levels including post-high school. However, the pioneers of the movement were especially interested in early childhood education and the pre-teen years of school, so most of the ideas that have now been applied at all levels were originally conceived for childhood education.

Goal Structure

Let's take a moment to examine the goal structure of the learner-centered curriculum. The goal is actually very clear, serving as a reminder of what really matters to learner-centered advocates: it is the goal of *self-realization*, or what the psychologist Abraham Maslow called *self- actualization*. What self-realization or self-actualization means as a goal of a curriculum is that the school experience should be such that each individual has the freedom and opportunity to aspire to what he or she dreams of becoming.

Freedom and opportunity, especially as they stand in contrast to the restraint and coercion so often identified with traditional schooling, are key concepts in learner centering. The teacher in a learner-centered curriculum accepts this clear goal of self-realization or self-actualization for each learner and establishes the goal structure accordingly. This means an environment in which opportunities for self-realization are abundant. This means meeting the needs and interests of the individual learner by giving the learner opportunities to explore, to follow his/her curiosities, and to exercise personal choice and responsibility. See Figure 5.1 for a listing of the salient features of learner-centered curriculum.

Figure 5.1. Keys to the Learner-Centered Curriculum

Emphasis	◆ Focus on the individual ◆ Personal growth and development ◆ Learner interest ◆ Emphasis on affect
Teaching	◆ Teacher as facilitator
Learning	◆ Incidental education
Environment	◆ Nurturing creativity ◆ Stimulating ◆ Playful atmosphere ◆ Freedom of movement ◆ Atmosphere of trust
Assessment	◆ Learner-initiated ◆ Growth oriented ◆ Formative emphasis ◆ Anecdotal, experiential ◆ Non competitive

The orientation of the learner-centered curriculum is found in the doctrine of interest, which states simply that students should study what they want to study. What and how does a student want to learn? What motivates a given individual? Are students, especially young ones, capable of knowing what they need and want to learn? How can a teacher know what interests an individual student might have? What experiences will best serve a learner's interests? How can the teacher facilitate the learner's growth toward self-realization? The focus of the learner-centered curriculum is indeed on the individual, the individual's dreams and goals and interests. Regarding the doctrine of interest, the philosopher Jean-Jacques Rousseau wrote that yes, "the student should study what he wants to study, but he should want to study what the teacher wants him to study." It would be easy to misconstrue Rousseau's statement as manipulative, but in fact he was underscoring the importance of a friendly, warm relationship between student and teacher. After all, the teacher is an adult whose experience and wisdom the learner should come to seek. Obviously, conditions of trust, empathy, interest, and support must be present to give Rousseau's statement full meaning.

The foundation or cornerstone of the learner-centered curriculum is that of individual growth and development. The individual rather than traditional academic subject matter is the focus of a learner-centered curriculum. This is not a curriculum of mathematics, science, history, etc., but a curriculum of interests and experiences. To the extent that academic subject matter is helpful in meeting learner interests and needs, it becomes a useful tool. But to think of academic subject matter from the separate disciplines as the basis of the curriculum is to misunderstand priorities. John Dewey noted that the learner and the curriculum are essentially one: the learner is the curriculum. From a learner-centered viewpoint, this insight by Dewey puts to rest the commonly held perception that the curriculum is an objectified entity, something separate from the learner. Let us look at a few examples of learner-centering to make the point.

Open Education

A number of years ago in the United States, a movement known as open education flourished, reaching its peak in the 1970s. Open education included everything from school architecture (classrooms without walls) to a curriculum of learner choice. The open approach to the curriculum included in particular a reaction to textbooks, organized scope and sequence, adult imposed subject matter, rigid discipline, and formal assessment. The idea, as suggested by the term *open*, is to allow students to choose their own course of study and to pursue those things that interest them most. The teacher's primary role is that of facilitating, not directing, student learning. Open education is described by Rogers and Freiberg (1994, p. 261) as follows:

> [It is] an open approach to the teaching-learning process which recognizes the valid wish of every student to be involved in some way in the direction of his own learning. It respects children's natural impulse to learn and understands the way they gain and create knowledge. Of special concern, it changes the function of a teacher from "telling information" to one of providing choice and facilitating inquiry activity.

What is rather obvious in the preceding quote is the movement of the center of gravity from teacher to learner, the emphasis on the individual's self-direction, and the legitimizing of his/her opportunity to make choices. Notice the emphasis on learner creativity and absence of such terms as basic skills, discipline, and teacher direction. Open education means a fluid, interest-based curriculum. The open education curriculum is a curriculum of freedom from restraint and expanded opportunity.

Articles began to surface in the 1970s pointing out the shortcomings of open education. Particularly persuasive were essays written by education editor Fred Hechinger, who authored a weekly column on education for the *New York Times*. Hechinger suggested that open schools were mainly places where students learned little of lasting importance and that they represented an experiment that had basically failed. This influential condemnation marked the beginning of the end of open education. However, in his meta-analysis of various educational strategies and programs, educational researcher Herbert Walberg (1984) concluded that the academic results of open education were in fact, quite comparable to those of traditional approaches. By the time this evidence was presented, however, it was far too late to resuscitate the open education movement, assuming there was the will to do so, but given the cyclical nature of American education, one can be sure that it will reappear clothed in different terminology and trappings.

A. S. Neill and Summerhill School

Learner-centered education was taken to its limits by the renowned Scottish educator, A. S. Neill. Neill founded, and operated for many years, a school in England known as Summerhill. It was Neill's feeling that the child is innately wise and good and perfectly capable of making right choices. He writes that most teachers "start out with the assumption that human nature is bad; I start out with the realization that human nature is good. That is the real distinction between the disciplinarian and the believer in freedom" (Neill 1917, p. 43).

Summerhill was, and continues to be, a school where students are given freedom of choice, including whether or not to attend classes, do assignments, or participate at all. Largely, individuals at Summerhill make their own decisions about their education. Its existential nature is legendary. Personal choice is everything. The individual is empowered to decide not merely what, but even whether to study. Given Neill's deep-seated belief in the fundamental goodness of human nature, the perception is that the choices individuals make are more typically good than not, and even in those instances where someone makes a mistake, the process of making decisions and reflecting on them is inevitably part of one's personal growth.

What happens to children who attended Summerhill? Do they learn anything of lasting value? A follow up study by Bernstein (1968; see also Montague in *Summerhill: For and Against* by Neill 1970, pp. 49–63) of 50 former students yielded a generally favorable impression of the experience.

Those who were disgruntled cited a lack of emphasis on academic subjects and lack of good teaching as their primary complaints. However, those who were satisfied felt that the school and the curriculum were proving grounds for the development of tolerance, sincerity, and generally healthy relationships with others. They also noted the opportunities for "natural" growth and development in line with personal interests and abilities.

Affective Education

Yet another example of a learner-centered approach to the curriculum is one known as affective education, that is, education that puts feelings, emotions, dreams, and aspirations ahead of other considerations such as basic skills and knowledge. This is not to say that basic skills and knowledge are considered trivial by those who advocate this approach to the curriculum; in fact, such enthusiasts will readily tell you that when affective factors are seriously taken into account as integral to the curriculum, achievement will follow. The fact remains, however, that in affective education the abiding focus is on the subjective, the intra- and interpersonal. Subject matter is seen as a useful tool in the exploration of values and decisions; for example, literary themes such as love, conflict, angst, compassion, pride, etc., are seen as beneficial to the extent that they enable individuals to reflect on their own lives and to find meaning as a result. As you might imagine, great emphasis is placed on the arts, creativity, and individual expression in an affective education curriculum.

The work of the humanistic psychologist, Carl Rogers (1969, 1994) was particularly influential in affective education. Rogers promoted a therapeutic approach to the curriculum, one in which the child's mental and emotional health is prominent. He set forth a curricular agenda aimed toward personal growth, participation based on interest, the joys of learning, all in a warm, supportive, nurturing environment. Rogers saw curriculum content as completely negotiable. People should learn what they want to learn. The key to a successful curricular experience, according to Rogers, is the establishment of seven educational priorities, including:

- a climate of trust,
- a participatory mode of decision making,
- helping students to prize themselves,
- uncovering the excitement of discovery learning,
- teachers acting as facilitators of learning,
- helping teachers themselves to grow as persons, and
- an awareness that the good life is within each of us.

Developmentally Appropriate Practice

Among the many permutations of the learner-centered curriculum is that known as *developmental education* or developmentally appropriate practice. Primary or kindergarten teachers are quite familiar with the term and with the key idea that a learner-centered classroom is one that begins neither with subject matter to be covered, nor with lists of academic outcomes, but with the learner. The teacher focuses on each learner at his or her state of growth and development. A developmentally appropriate curriculum is one that caters to the developmental level and interests of each and every learner. This can happen only when the teacher becomes a caring observer of his/her students. In other words, the teacher's first task is to study the students, to learn their likes and dislikes, their levels of maturity, their strengths and weaknesses. Developmentally appropriate practice demands of the teacher that he/she know the whole child because the child is the key to the curriculum. Put another way, and paraphrasing Dewey, the child and the curriculum are one.

One curricular example of developmentally appropriate practice is the use of learning centers in the classroom, a practice more commonly associated with early and primary education, although it need not be limited to those age levels. Centers are located strategically around the room, and children are encouraged to visit and become engaged at those centers that are of interest to them. Typically, centers roughly approximate school subjects, so one would normally expect to find in such a classroom a reading center, mathematics center, and centers that feature the arts, games, social studies, and science, among others.

An intriguing variant of the centers approach is one described to me by a graduate student who had visited a primary (elementary) school in England. The school had arranged the curriculum so that different classrooms in the building corresponded to different school subjects. There was a mathematics room, an art room, a reading/language room, a geography room, and so on. The students would sign up, based on interest, to visit various rooms. Teachers were assigned to classrooms based on their own interests, and were present to facilitate students' inquiry and projects. This approach to learner-centering made it possible to house supplies and materials related to specific subject matter in convenient locations. The program was one of integrated studies, so that when a child was in the mathematics room, for example, he/she would use mathematics to the extent that it was helpful in working on some particular problem or investigation.

The centers approach is considered developmentally appropriate because, among other reasons, it allows teachers more time to observe students, to listen and talk with them about their interests, and to help individuals with ideas and materials in order to facilitate their inquiry. Very little frontal, whole-class teaching takes place, and children are encouraged to take the initiative as they decide what, when, and how to study. A classroom where interest centers are present is a classroom where issues such as personal responsibility, respect for property, and respect for the rights of others arise quite naturally along the way. Although the centers approach is typically associated with early education, a variant known as "stations" has been successfully used with older students, for example, in a biology lab, a physical education class, or in any other subject where the teacher and students decide that this approach is viable.

The Doctrine of Interest

Tied to the idea of individual aspiration is the controversial idea known as the doctrine of interest. It is an old idea, one that goes back at least to the 1st Century A.D., a Roman educator, Quintilian, introduced the doctrine of interest, explaining it in the following way. He wrote that students ought to study what they want to study. In other words, the curriculum should be built on student interest. Quintilian argued that forcing students to learn things they are not particularly interested in is largely a waste of everyone's time. Such learning goes in one ear and out the other, so the saying goes. According to the doctrine of interest, teachers need to find out what students are interested in and support them in these interests. The idea is actually so old as to predate Quintilian by a few centuries. Plato alluded to it when he wrote that you can make someone stronger, even against their will, by enforcing physical exercise, but that you cannot force the mind to learn.

To be sure, it takes a great deal of faith in childhood sensibility and in a child's ability to determine what he/she needs to accept the doctrine of interest fully. The idea itself is maddeningly simple: one needs to find out what students are interested in, individually and collectively and help them with their interests. But in order to do this, one must study one's students. As Susan Isaacs, a psychologist who worked at the Malting House School in England in the 1920s wrote, "The key to the school is the growth of the children, and its methods must be based on direct observation of the children themselves. One of the most far-reaching changes of thought in human history is the modern view of the freedom of children as the basis of education. This is the great experiment of our age." (quoted in *Neill of Summerhill*, by Jonathan Croall, 1983, p. 162). If, as Isaacs thought, the "freedom of children" is to be the basis of education, then the doctrine of interest must be the guiding premise.

Creativity and Self-Direction

Another aspect of learner-centered classrooms is that they are places where creativity is continually encouraged. Inevitably, one finds considerable emphasis on the arts, music, drama, and various avenues of creative expression. After all, it is in the idiosyncratic, personalized notion of what is beautiful, appropriate, and meaningful that students find meaning in life. In the learner-centered curriculum, it is incumbent upon the teacher to establish the conditions for learning so that individual creativity can flower. Childhood creativity, so the feeling goes, is best encouraged by the teacher who is, in the phrase of psychologist Abraham Maslow, a "helpful let-be." The term speaks for itself. Creativity suffers from excessive adult surveillance, from rigid assignments, from restriction of movement, from expected and enforced conformity and docility and from overly-critical evaluation. It flowers in environments of openness, support, sharing, and caring. These are fundamental tenets of learner-centering.

Jean Piaget could well be described as a minimalist, someone who preferred to let students learn on their own with little direct adult intervention. He described teaching as the establishment of environments where meaningful learning could emerge. In that sense, the teacher's work in establishing the curriculum is environmental. The teacher creates a stimulating environment in which students are free to explore and to come to terms first hand with physical, social, and logical knowledge. Physical knowledge comes from sensory learning, from hands-on experience. Social knowledge comes from interaction with others, where students learn give and take, cooperation and competition, where they learn from direct experience that others, too, have needs. Logical knowledge is built as students assimilate new information, accommodate pre-existing knowledge to new ideas, and strive toward equilibrium as the world within and without emerges in consciousness.

The teacher plays three crucial roles: that of organizer of the learning environment, assessor of children's thinking, and initiator of group activities, including games and discussions. Piaget noted in his writings more than once that the best learning is always spontaneous, and nothing has a sense of spontaneity that can compare with play. The environment, therefore, must be playful in all that idea entails. Play is the ascendance of engagement over outcome, of activity over passivity, and of natural interest over coercion. True play is always spontaneous, unscripted, and never other-directed.

Also found in a learner-centered curriculum is the notion of self-direction. Always present is the idea that the learner decides. The center of gravity is found with the learner, not with textbook, teacher, or prescribed course of study. Growth comes through self-direction, decision making, self-reflection, and self-assessment. Accompanying the notion of self-direction is the idea that most meaningful learning in a child centered or learner centered curriculum comes through discovery. And the main discovery is not so much the discovery of knowledge external to the learner, but self-discovery: a continuous process of discovering who you are and who you are becoming.

Syntactic Complexity

Advocates of learner-centered approaches argue that such environments are more syntactically complex than traditional environments. A syntactically complex learning environment is the opposite of one dominated by seatwork, textbooks, worksheets, and isolation. Instead, it is an environment where learners are given freedom of movement and opportunities to succeed and fail. Typically, it is a project-oriented environment where students explore ideas and experience the give and take of working with others. It means indirect forms of instruction and a focus on problems: social problems, personal problems, intellectual problems. In such environments, you find students talking to each other, working together and alone, and an emphasis on experience over teacher-directed lessons. As a result, one finds an integrated focus to the curriculum. The school subjects are present, to be sure, but not so much in a direct sense. Rather, they play the role of tools, not that of ends in themselves. The point is that students trying to solve higher level problems, do higher level thinking, and deal with complex issues of working together, often utilize formal subjects as a means, one very useful tool for solving problems.

The teacher gets off center stage. Teachers do less talking and less directing. The locus of control is with the learner, not with the teacher. The teacher's role is to support, to nurture, to diagnose, to find out what students' real interests are and to support the pursuit of those interests along the way. The teacher is there to mediate when necessary. Much of the teacher's time is spent listening and talking with individuals about their work. The teacher becomes a student of his/her students. It is expected that teachers in learner-centered classrooms will know their students well.

Summing Up

As you can imagine, in a learner-centered curriculum, much emphasis is on what John Dewey and others have called incidental education and collateral learning, that is, the things that happen along the way. For example, consider the things that occur spontaneously when two children want to use the same piece of equipment at the same time. The potential for genuine growth and development can emerge from such a moral dilemma. Consider the incidental education that comes about through an interest-centered classroom where students learn from experience that sometimes you win games and sometimes you lose games. For students learning to play chess, participation means more than having your own way and winning all the time.

The learner-centered curriculum takes into account things that happen in context, the sort of social/moral growth made possible when people are free to make choices. Consider if you will, students working together on a science project. It is expected that they will learn certain science knowledge, but just listen to them as they work together. They talk about what they are doing, they question each other, they make plans, the assess along the way. Such an example provides insight to the essential keys of a learner centered curriculum, particularly that it cannot be scripted with behavioral objectives because it takes on the natural flow of life where individuals are allowed to follow their interests.

Let us summarize the key elements of learner-centering in the curriculum. Learner interest is the cornerstone. Yet, 20 centuries after its introduction by Quintilian, the doctrine of interest still holds little sway. Many teachers simply do not believe that students are capable of identifying and studying the things they really need. There is the fear that students will leave out important areas that later in life they may well wish they had concentrated on. Finally, it is a matter of trust, whether teachers feel they can trust students to choose their own learning experiences. These are not simple issues, easily dismissed either by advocates or detractors of learner-centering.

Closely related to the doctrine of interest is the matter of locus of control. In learner-centered programs, the locus of control resides ideally with the learner. Students learn what they live. The argument is that if they are given choices, then they can experience the responsibility of living with their choices. This is how meaningful growth is possible.

A learner-centered curriculum is relational. The relationships that develop between learner and teacher and among learners are prized as integral to the school experience. As a learner begins to become more self-aware, he/she is able to link that self-awareness to an awareness of others. Self awareness means awareness of self in the context of others and their needs. Such learning is thought by learner-centered enthusiasts to be as significant as learning academic knowledge and skills. Friendship and collaborative relationships can and will emerge in an environment of freedom, choice, and opportunity. The emphasis on social and moral experience is fundamental, and the spontaneous nature of learner-centered environments creates context for growth and development.

A learner-centered curriculum is certainly an idiosyncratic curriculum. You will not find a well crafted scope and sequence, because it is based on interests. Careful teacher observation is a key to determining student interest.

An interest-based curriculum is an evolving, emerging curriculum. Complexities arise given the focus on problem solving and discovery, as opposed to seatwork and compliance to arbitrary rules. Therefore, the curriculum has a tentative, emergent quality, the quality of life being lived.

A learner-centered curriculum is typically a curriculum of discovery. Discovery of the wider world is at stake to be sure, but equally important is the journey of self- discovery that leads to self-realization. Such a curriculum is non-linear, emergent, seemingly unstructured, and often unpredictable.

Your Turn

You, the reader, are invited to participate in this venture. Take a moment before visiting several exemplars of the learner-centered curriculum to jot down what has occurred to you so far.

Ask yourself the most basic of reflective questions before you continue your tour of curriculum.

- ◆ How has it reinforced what you already knew?
- ◆ Are there any tensions between what you thought before and what you are beginning to think is possible?

Learner-Centered Curriculum Exemplars

Three learner-centered exemplars are presented here: Sudbury Schools; The Exploratory Experiences Curriculum for Elementary Schools (EECES); and Reggio Emilia Education. They differ in their development and their characteristics, but share an emphasis on the individual child's interests and growth.

Sudbury Schools

A Learner-Centered and Learner-Controlled Approach

What flight and air are to the bird, play is to the child.

Susan Blow

The child should study what he wants to study.

Quintilian, 1st Century A.D.

The doctrine of interest is alive and well at Sudbury Schools. So learner-centered are these schools that they claim not to have a curriculum. Everything is based on learner choice. If a student wants to learn about insects, then that becomes his/her course of study for the nonce. The staff are there to facilitate and enable the learner's quest in any way they can, but the emphasis is on learning and study, not on teaching and direction.

Sudbury schools are a loosely connected network of independent schools that adhere to the philosophy of the original Sudbury Valley School, founded in Sudbury, Massachusetts in 1968. The schools are mutually supportive of one another, but each school operates as an independent entity, subscribing to the philosophy of childhood freedom, natural curiosity, choice, and personal responsibility.

Sudbury schools lay claim to being "hands-on" democracies. The schools are managed by the weekly School Meeting, where every student and staff member has a vote. Everyone is empowered, even to the point of hiring and/or dismissing school staff. All decisions of any consequence are taken up at the School Meetings. The model is similar to that of the direct democracy practiced in the Swiss cantons, or in the tradition of the New England Town Hall Meetings. This is site-based management taken to the ultimate level.

Student and Teacher Roles

At Sudbury Schools, kids choose for themselves what to do all day, every day. Students group together naturally around common interests. Classes are organized only on the basis of student interest. Achievement is measured by the students themselves. Grades are not a factor. These statements are taken more or less verbatim from the website of Chicago Sudbury School (www. chicagosudburyschool.org).

◆ They speak clearly to where the center of gravity is found, that is, with the learner.

◆ Teachers are there to facilitate student learning, to be sure, but their role is not that of director, teller, manager, or anything like a traditional teacher role.

Sudbury schools are not age-graded. Students are simply students at the school. In anything approach a traditional sense, there is no curriculum. There is no scope and sequence. There is no set of required courses because there are no courses. Learner interest guides the experience. Students study what they want to study. The idea is that no one knows what any given individual needs to learn more than the individual him/herself. Therefore, there is an underlying foundation of trust in the judgment of the child to choose those things he/she wants to learn. This would strike hard-core traditional curriculum advocates as license more than liberty. Certainly those who do not trust young people to decide for themselves what they should learn will have trouble with this model.

Sudbury schools claim they are putting American ideals back into education. Ideals such as freedom, democracy, and rule by law are basic to the Sudbury experience. Even though students at a typical Sudbury school range in age from four to nineteen years, everyone is included in decision making, opportunities to choose what to study, and how to spend the day in general. Beyond required attendance, the experience is entirely elective. The question will arise, "what if a child chooses not to study anything?" The Sudbury response is that such a choice is up to the child, but that, given the stimulating environment and the atmosphere of support, it tends not to be a problem of any lasting concern.

In Sudbury schools, children of mixed ages learn to go about their work and play, following a naturalistic path of education in the sense that no prescribed curriculum, no set of standards, no required examinations exist. Students choose each day what to do and how to spend their time. Formal classes are rare and are organized only on student request.

Assessment is largely a matter of self-assessment. Students decide for themselves how much they have learned. They decide for themselves how to know how much they have learned. Because there is no predetermined curriculum, it is impossible to have "one size fits all" assessments, particularly in some standardized form. The intent is away from standardization and centralization of authority, so it would make little sense, given the Sudbury philosophy, to do any kind of formal testing.

The Big Rock Sudbury School Model

The Big Rock Sudbury School (marinsudbury.org) offers six points of school philosophy. While they are noted as cornerstones of the Big Rock Sudbury School, they are typical of Sudbury philosophy in general.

◆ *Independent Study*

Students are encouraged to be guided by their natural curiosity and pursue their real passions. Through the power of free will children learn faster and magnitudes deeper. Generally, mastering a regular school subject takes a fraction of the time it takes in a traditional coercive school environment.

◆ *Age Mixing*

Students and staff freely associate by interest. People of different ages bring different perspectives, skills, and experience to enhance each other's development. Practicing cooperation and mutual respect, students develop a strong sense of supporting and caring for each other.

◆ *Self-Evaluation and Feedback*

As each student is bound to pursue a unique and special course through life in this fast changing modern society, self-evaluation and feedback from peers and adults are far more useful to learning than artificial grading systems.

◆ *Democratic Governance*

The school is run by the School Meeting, in which students and staff members have equal votes. It passes the rules governing daily operation, budget, and hiring. Here students learn about real life as they participate and have power in an authentic democracy. This is hard and important work where kids have responsibility to help make real policy decisions. This process is the key difference from other schools where kids are assigned artificial exercises, governed by adults and thereby separated from real life learning.

◆ *Due Process*

When disputes arise, the issues are resolved through fair public process by students and staff through the Judicial Committee. There is no fear of teachers or adults. Students learn to solve conflicts eye-to-eye, and that justice in a democracy belongs to everyone.

◆ *Role of Staff*

Staff at Sudbury schools are attentive and resourceful but at the same time not directive and coercive. By truly respecting children, adults earn genuine respect in return. This crucial relationship of cooperation and trust creates a nurturing environment that is unique to Sudbury schools.

The reader will note similarities between these statements of purpose and the philosophy of A. S. Neill's Summerhill School, considered at the time (Summerhill was founded in 1921) to be a radical approach to childhood education. Self-governance, freedom of choice, and a "naturalistic" approach to learning are educational concepts held in common by Summerhill and Sudbury.

Note also the use of key progressive terms (in spite of the fact that Sudbury distinguishes itself from progressive schools) such as *natural curiosity, interest, experience, democracy, nurture, relationship.* And finally, please note that Sudbury Schools follow the tendency of other distinctive educational programs to define themselves not merely by what they are, but by what they are not.

Your Turn

- ◆ What are some points of agreement and disagreement that you hold in regard to the Sudbury approach?

The Exploratory Experiences Curriculum for Elementary Schools

An Interest Center Approach

Experience is the child of Thought, and Thought is the child of Action.

Benjamin Disraeli

The Exploratory Experiences Curriculum for Elementary Schools (EECES) is a learner-centered curriculum that uses interest centers as its focus. The philosophy of EECES is that each child develops in unique ways according to his/her interests. The term "interest" is invariably identified with progressive education, sending a clear signal that the curriculum must fit the child, not the other way around. Interest, however, is not to be confused with superficial curiosity. Rather, it represents the deep-seated inclinations of individuals who are differentially drawn to those things they truly care about. In a curriculum based on interest, the individual child becomes the center of gravity, making decisions about what to study and how best to study it. The emphasis is upon "study" as opposed to instruction. The child, not the teacher or text, initiates inquiry.

A common misconception is that such a curriculum borders on academic anarchy, and that immature children who have little idea of what they really need to know in order to succeed in life are being allowed to dictate their learning. At its worst, this is probably so. The counter argument offered up by EECES is that a purposeful, enriching learning environment is the key. In other words, the choices students make about what to study are choices made within a carefully selected range of options. The options are established in the form of interest centers that students visit as their interests dictate.

The Interest Centers Approach

The interest centers correspond rather closely to school subjects, and they typically include the following:

- *The Reading Center* occupies a corner of the classroom and contains a small library consisting of a couple of shelves of books and magazines, a carpet, several pillows, and a rocking chair.

- *The Science Center* contains science inquiry materials for students to study. The materials change over time, for example, solids and liquids, rocks and minerals, insect study, plants, gadgets and electronics, astronomy, etc.

- *The Mathematics Center* has manipulative materials of different kinds, mathematical problems and activities, basic skills exercises, and certain games that teach quantitative concepts.

- *The Games Center* has games such as checkers, chess, other board games, and a variety of puzzles and problem solving activities. Often in the case of older students, tournaments are held, clubs formed, etc.

- *The Art Center* features art activities including painting, drawing, sculpting, architecture, etc. The corner features a particular theme each month, and students are encouraged to express themselves artistically in ways that illustrate the theme.

- *The World Center* has maps and graphics, biographies, histories, geography activities, and pictures. Students explore time and space with an emphasis on their own role as historians and geographers.

- *The Theater Center* has puppet theater, musical instruments, play scripts, and socio-drama activities. Students are encouraged to become involved in expressing themselves through dramatic play, role play, theater production, and musical expression.

Most classrooms are rather crowded places with little room for extras. Therefore, each "center" is often little more than a table, a counter top, or a corner of the room. The centers remain up throughout the year, and they tend to change themes with the seasons, with the course of study, and with emphasis on special topics of local interest. An example of this is the involvement of students in a successful attempt to help with the reclamation of a salmon stream. The various centers focused to the extent that it was reasonable during that time on topics related to the theme.

To ensure developmentally appropriate practice, the center content in a given school varies according to age and/or grade level. The curriculum uses the spiral concept in which topics are visited and revisited throughout the elementary years at increasing levels of sophistication. Thus older students are regularly called on to help in primary classes who are studying the same topic.

Student and Teacher Roles

Each student decides what centers to visit for what purposes. Students keep a log of their visits and are encouraged to reflect on their choices. As a means of controlling access and in the name of fairness, students sign up to use particular centers. When a center is fully subscribed, then a student must select another center. Typically, students are allowed to sign up for a given center for a period of two or three days. Each student is encouraged to use all the centers, and part of the teacher's role is to ensure that this happens. If problems arise, and they inevitably will, the issues are discussed either during contemporary living or during reflection time. Such problems are viewed as a meaningful activity for student discussion because they provide grist for social/moral decision making.

The teacher's role is turned inside out and upside down in this curriculum. It typically takes some getting used to. Very little direct instruction happens except during the 60 minutes per day allotted to basic skills, which mainly involves reading, writing, and mathematics (the 3 Rs). One veteran first grade teacher who used this curriculum volunteered that although she had taught for years, she felt that she had gotten to know her students better using the EECES approach than she had ever known her students before. The teacher's role is usually one of listening, acting as arbiter, discussing issues with an individual or small group, helping with materials, or lending a guiding hand at an appropriate moment.

The EECES Schedule

The EECES curriculum divides the 300-minute school day into various blocks of time, each of which is treated rather fluidly depending on student interest and teacher judgment. This schedule remains throughout the elementary grades, and it is halved in the case of half-day kindergarten except for literature and reflection time which remain about the same length. Explanations of the blocks of time follow. Please note that the time blocks are rather approximate, simply because it is impossible to predict levels of interest and need for more or less time on any given day.

- *Contemporary Living* (15–30 minutes) comes first in the morning. It involves routines such as attendance, singing, flag salute, and lunch count as well as any significant announcements, show and tell, and brief discussions of topics of interest to the class. This is considered to be a crucial block of time because it sets the tone for the day. It is a key to this curriculum that a relaxed, informal, supportive atmosphere is created as the students begin their daily activities.

- *Free Time* (60–120 minutes)—It has long been argued that one of the things adults need to learn is how to use their leisure time wisely. Given the statistics on television viewing, apparently many of them have not figured out other alternatives. EECES curriculum deems free time important because 1) it gives students the opportunity to make decisions and follow through on them and 2) it puts the student in control of his/her time, a valuable experience that transfers to out of school and beyond. The purpose of this block is to give students practice in the meaningful use of leisure time. Students are given a full hour each morning to use the various centers. They sign up in advance for a given center, and they are free to conduct themselves in any meaningful way during this time. The teacher roams the room, providing assistance, support, arbitration, listening to plans, whatever is needed. Students read, write, do art work, work on projects, play games, and generally become involved in the content of the centers.

- *Performing Arts/Humanities* (30+ minutes)—This block of time is devoted to creative expression in the form of skits, dancing, poetry reading, dramatic play, theater, singing, and other performance activities. Especially encouraged is original work by the students.

- *Literature* (15+ minutes)—During this time the teacher reads to the class from works of literary merit. Books and stories chosen must past the test of being beyond the independent reading level of most of the students and of a nature that is uplifting and purposeful. Typically literature time is right after lunch recess and is little different from the time-tested story-time that teachers have used for years.

- *Problem Solving/Inquiry* (60–120 minutes)—This time block focuses on whole-class problem solving, typically in the form of an integrated studies unit. The idea is to bring the entire class together to work on a common theme. These thematic units generally last two to four weeks and are designed to incorporate language arts, social studies, science, mathematics, the arts, and other subjects as tools for solving problems. This time block often shows linkages with Free Time, and it is not unusual to see students working on the unit theme either independently or in small groups during Free Time. The teacher plays the role of facilitator and guide, assisting the class in a multitude of ways. An example of a problem solving unit was one in which the class grew various plants from seeds and cuttings, performing simple experiments, constructing small greenhouses, conducting soil studies, making plant containers, linking up with a nearby plant nursery for guidance, studying the local flora, and actually holding a community sale of the plants the students grew during the unit. Because the thematic units are complex and involve nearly every subject of the curriculum, it is necessary to marshal the entire class, often working in committees, to sustain the effort. Part of the teacher's role is to ensure that everyone plays a part in the effort from planning the unit to the reflective assessment that serves as an ongoing guide throughout the process.

- *Movement/Physical Education* (30+ minutes)—This is a time devoted to physical exercise, games, and other activities that demand participation. Emphasis is placed on cooperation and competition as well as on team and individual activity.

- *Recess* (15 minutes morning and afternoon)—Recess belongs completely to the students and is considered to be a true break from the routine. It is a time of play, relaxation, friendship, and in some cases, sleep.

Curricular Balance

Because students decide for themselves what they will study, the issue of curricular balance, or more often the issue of curricular imbalance, becomes a logical point of concern. In a traditional curriculum, students are exposed to the entire range of subject. Adults decide for them how much time is devoted to mathematics, reading, etc. In the EECES curriculum, the equation is turned around: individuals decide how much time they will devote to reading, mathematics, etc. However, two subtle factors crucial to the curriculum's success are at work.

- *Purposeful Choices*

  The first of these is the democratic idea of choices within a purposeful framework. The centers basically represent school subjects, so that the entire traditional curriculum is in fact present. Student choices are made with respect to which centers to visit. Allowing the student to choose provides opportunity for taking responsibility and for making meaningful choices. It also creates a changed psychology of curriculum because the student has chosen to study something as opposed to a situation in which this is dictated by others.

- *Teacher as Nurturer*

  The second factor is the nurturing role of the teacher who finds far more time than a traditional teacher-directed curriculum affords to listen to and talk with individuals about their interests; to support them in their inquiry, and to offer guidance from a caring, responsible adult. If a student consistently shuns the mathematics center, the teacher is presented with an opportunity to find out why this is so. It may have little to do with an aversion to mathematics but merely to the way it is presented or perceived to be presented by the student. Student interest is often sparked by the teacher who in a relational context is able to introduce possibilities the student could not have imagined on his/her own.

Finally, however, balance is seldom achieved in any curriculum, no matter how it is structured. Students find dozens of ways of avoiding real learning even when we force "balance" upon them. It has been known at least since Plato's time that you cannot force the mind to learn those things it does not want to learn. The EECES' argument is that when students are allowed to follow their interests in a rich, nurturing environment, they will learn to make meaningful choices. It has been argued for years that children must be told to eat their vegetables or they will not grow up to be big and strong. It has also been argued that given the opportunity to select their own diet within a range of healthy options, children will indeed eat the foods they need. This debate will continue.

Please note that the EECES curriculum does not represent any specific curriculum project, commercial or noncommercial. Rather, it is typical of the longstanding progressive education child-centered interest centers approach. Invariably, when it is put into practice in a given school, local modifications are implemented. Many of the ideas of EECES, although they are clearly typical of hundreds of progressive early childhood and elementary school projects, are based on the work of Professors Harlan and Ruth Hansen of the University of Minnesota, who devoted much of their careers to the theory and practice and child-centered teaching and learning.

Your Turn

Some curriculum models focus on secondary schools; some are devoted to young children.

- ◆ Are there any characteristics that you think are common to all students K–12?

Exemplar 3

Reggio Emilia Education

A Project-Based Child-Centered Community Approach

Creativity becomes more visible when adults try to be more attentive to the cognitive processes of children than to the results
they achieve in various fields of doing and understanding.

Loris Malaguzzi

Description and Brief History

The Reggio Emilia approach is based on the early childhood education
programs developed in the town of Reggio Emilia, Italy. For more than four
decades, this small wealthy community has dedicated a generous portion of
its budget to provide high quality childcare for children six years of age and
younger. The approach is a blend of constructivist and progressive educational practices, with experiential, exploratory learning at the center. The
stated goal of Reggio Emilia, which reflects an attempt to avoid Italy's unfortunate 20th Century fascist history, is to help children "acquire skills of critical thinking and collaboration essential to rebuilding and ensuring a
democratic society" (New 2000, p. 1).

The system is based on the work of its founder, Loris Malaguzzi
(1920–1994) and upon the Italian accepted cultural norm that children are the
collective responsibility of the community (New 1993). Malaguzzi aimed to
make Reggio Emilia a place of research, learning, revisiting, reconsideration,
and reflection. In the Reggio Emilia curriculum, consistent attempts are made
"to ensure that every child feels a sense of belonging within the school community and to strengthen each child's sense of identity as an individual"
(Edmiaston & Fitzgerald 2000, p. 66). A guiding premise is the shared belief
that children have "an innate understanding of how to relate to the world"
(Bennett 2001, p. 2). Malaguzzi believed in a curriculum in which children express their understanding through a wide variety of symbolic and graphic
means, including speech, writing, movement, drawing, painting, building,
sculpture, shadow play, collage, dramatic play, and music. This is all a part of
what Malaguzzi called "the hundred languages of children."

Reggio Emilia employs four key principles:

- encouraging collaborative relationships with other children and adults,
- constructing effective environments for learning and growth,
- developing project-based curriculum experiences, and
- documenting learning in multiple ways (Edmiaston & Fitzgerald 2000, p. 66).

Therefore, an observer should expect to see children learning together in stimulating, practical settings where projects are undertaken and where assessment flows naturally from experience.

The East Tennessee State University Center for Childhood Learning and Development lists eight characteristics of the Reggio Emilia approach:

1. *The image of the child:* all children have potential, construct their own learning, and are capable.
2. *Community and system:* children, family, teachers, parents, and community are interactive and work together.
3. *Interest in environment and beauty:* school and classrooms are beautiful places.
4. *Collaboration by teachers:* teams, partners, working together, sharing information, sharing in projects.
5. *Time not set by clock:* respect for children's pace/time table, stay with teachers for several years, and relationships remain constant.
6. *Emergent curriculum/projects:* child-entered, follows childhood interests, returning again and again (spiral curriculum) to add new insights.
7. *Environmental stimulation:* encourages activity, involvement, discovery, and use of a variety of media.
8. *Documentation:* observing, recording, thinking, and showing children's learning.

Curriculum

The curriculum is based on student interest and "is characterized by many features advocated by contemporary research on young children, including real-life problem solving among peers, with numerous opportunities for creative thinking and exploration" (New 1993, p. 2). Reggio Emilia is not a formal curriculum. Teachers neither follow a predetermined scope and sequence, nor do they provide focused instruction in reading and writing (Edwards 2002). Instead, "classroom activities are set up to provide opportuni-

Reggio Emilia

ties for children to work with a variety of peers in collaborative small group contexts." (Edmiaston & Fitzgerald 2000, p. 67). It is common for teachers to work on long-term, open-ended projects with small groups of children while the rest of the class engages in a variety of activities typical of preschool classrooms (New 1993).

Although teachers work within a framework of general educational goals, they do not provide the specific purposes for projects. Teaching and learning are viewed as "negotiated, emergent processes between adults and children, involving generous time and in-depth revisiting and reviewing" (Edwards 2002, pp. 5–6). Project topics originate with teacher observations of student interest. This means that teachers must know their students well. Teachers facilitate student learning by introducing materials and opportunities for students to explore topics of interest. New (1993, p. 2) writes:

> The topic of investigation may derive directly from teacher observations of children's spontaneous play and exploration. Project topics are also selected on the basis of academic curiosity or social concern on the part of teachers or parents, or serendipitous events that direct the attention of the children and teachers. Reggio teachers place a high value on their ability to improvise and respond to children's predisposition to enjoy the unexpected. Regardless of their origins, successful projects are those that generate a sufficient amount of interest and uncertainty to provoke children's creative thinking and problem solving and are open to different avenues of exploration.

The organizational structure of Reggio Emilia contributes to curricular planning. Teams of two teachers divide responsibilities for each class, with one teacher observing and documenting student interactions. Curricular decisions are based on shared observations among teachers, parents, and curricular specialists. So, each school is staffed with two teachers per classroom, an administrator who reports directly to the town council, and an *atelierista* (a teacher trained in the arts who works with classroom teachers in curriculum development and documentation), and several auxiliary staff. The environment itself is known as the "third teacher." Special attention is paid to the organization of the physical environment to ensure that classrooms are integrated with one another and that the school is integrated with the community (New 1993, pp. 1–2).

Teacher and Student Roles

Malaguzzi was convinced that children have an "innate understanding of how to relate to the world" (Bennett 2001, p. 2). Therefore, they are invited to "become researchers in the classrooms… by learning to ask questions and collect data with which to answer them" (Bennett 2001, p. 2). The role of the teacher is supportive, nurturing, and facilitating, in other words anything to enable children to grow in confidence and to enjoy their learning. This can happen only to the extent that teachers know and care about their students. Teachers also are expected to build bridges to parents and community, and to involve them in the life of the school.

The term "relationship" continually comes to the fore in Reggio Emilia. Emphasis is placed on the idea of "each child in relation to others" with "reciprocal relationships with other children, family, teachers, society, and environment" (Edwards 2002). Teachers work modeling positive responses to others and by emphasizing the classroom as community (Edmiaston & Fitzgerald 2000). Parents are especially expected to participate in the life of the school and to help make decisions concerning school policies, curriculum planning and assessment, and child welfare.

Assessment

Reggio Emilia encourages the documentation of learning in a variety of ways, just as one might expect given Malaguzzi's philosophy of the "hundred languages of children." Documentation focuses on "children's experiences, memories, thoughts, and ideas in the course of the work" and typically includes observations, transcriptions of tape-recordings, and photographs, such as these (Katz & Chard 1996):

- samples of a child's work at several different stages of completion;
- photographs showing work in progress and of children discussing their work;
- transcriptions of children's discussions, comments, and explanations of intentions about the activity; and
- comments made by parents and written by the teacher or other adults working with the children.

Obviously, the emphasis is on authentic assessment procedures. Given the fact that Reggio Emilia is an early childhood program, formal tests and related means of assessment would have little value in the documentation of student learning. Teacher judgment, student assessment, and student performance are the keys to assessment.

Summing Up

These exemplars of the Learner-Centered Curriculum focus on the self-realization of the individual learner. But they also address the environment and interactions of the students and teachers. To some extent, the difference between a learner-centered curriculum and one that is society-centered is one of degree as much as it is one of kind. Thus we turn our attention to another strand of curriculum exemplars that reveal progressive roots, those where the emphasis is primarily on social action.

Your Turn

First take the time to solidify your own thoughts about curriculum, having now examined the progressive paradigm, learner-centered curriculum, and several exemplars based on them. Write down what you think is important to include in each of the key components. If you like, write down thoughts about how this compares with the experience you have had as a teacher and as a student.

Don't worry about agreeing or disagreeing with any of the exemplars. Each of them was inspired by particular circumstances and philosophy. Your circumstances and philosophy will guide you.

- ◆ My ideal curriculum would include emphasis on…
- ◆ My ideal curriculum would include a teacher who…
- ◆ My ideal curriculum would include students who learn by…
- ◆ My ideal curriculum would include an environment characterized by…
- ◆ My ideal curriculum would include assessment based on …

In his book, *The Aims of Education*, the philosopher and mathematician Alfred North Whitehead (1929) attempted to address the central reasons for sending children to school. One idea, he suggested, is more basic than any other: "the students are alive, and the purpose of education is to stimulate and guide their self-development." The following excerpt is from Chapter One of the book.

> In training a child to activity of thought, above all things we must beware of what I will call "inert ideas"—that is to say, ideas that are merely received into the mind without being utilized, or tested, or thrown into fresh combinations.

> In the history of education, the most striking phenomenon is that schools of learning, which at one epoch are alive with a ferment of genius, in a succeeding generation exhibit merely pedantry and routine. The reason is that they are overladen with inert ideas. Education with inert ideas is not only useless: it is above all things, harmful.…

> Let us now ask how in our system of education we are to guard against this mental dryrot. We enunciate two educational commandments, *Do not teach too many subjects*, and again, *What you teach, teach thoroughly.*

The result of teaching small parts of a large number of subjects is the passive reception of disconnected ideas, not illumined with any spark of vitality. Let the main ideas which are introduced into a child's education be few and important, and let them be thrown into every combination possible.... Pedants sneer at an education which is useful. But if education is not useful, what is it? Is it a talent, to be hidden away in a napkin? Of course, education should be useful, whatever your aim in life....

Education is the acquisition of the art of the utilization of knowledge. This is an art very difficult to impart. Whenever a textbook is written of real educational worth, you may be quite certain that some reviewer will say that it will be difficult to teach from it. If it were easy, the book ought to be burned; for it cannot be educational.... And may I say in passing that no educational system is possible unless every question directly asked of a pupil at any examination is either framed or modified by the actual teacher of that pupil in that subject.

...What education has to impart is an intimate sense for the power of ideas, for the beauty of ideas, and for the structure of ideas, together with a particular body of knowledge which has peculiar reference to the life of the being possessing it.

Alfred North Whitehead (1929)

6

The Society-Centered Curriculum

Democratic communities help students to be as well as to become. They seek to help students meet their needs today as
well as become tomorrow's caring and active citizens.

Thomas Sergiovanni

Bringing democracy to life in the classroom requires that students have a genuine say in the curriculum and that their say
count for something.

James Beane

By the 1930s, the progressive educational movement had split into two distinctly different camps, one focused on the individual child as learner and the other focusing on the society at large as educational laboratory. The latter group viewed young people as idealistic: ready and capable of reforming society if the proper curricular leadership were provided. This meant a curriculum that reaches out beyond the classroom walls, into the community where students and teachers could change the world.

We will consider the society-centered curriculum in this chapter. We'll compare and contrast it both to the learner-centered curriculum presented earlier and to the knowledge-centered curriculum, which we have yet to encounter. And as you reflect on the meanings and applications of these three models, I have no illusion that you are or will become completely devoted to any one to the exclusion of the other two. My guess is that you will reach the conclusion that the society-centered curriculum, like the other two, has its specific strengths and weaknesses.

It is more likely that you will find in yourself and in your own experience a preference for certain elements of each. We do indeed have our tendencies, even our passions. Do you tend to be more knowledge-centered? learner-centered? society- centered? Few of us are purists. More often, we take the well-traveled road of eclecticism. Teachers and students live in a world of practice, and typically we are drawn to what seems to work best for us. Abraham Lincoln said it best, "People who like that kind of thing find that's just the kind of thing they like."

The goal structure of the society-centered curriculum is to explore and solve societal issues. Have you ever found yourself saying or thinking that you'd like to get the kids out into the real world to solve real-world problems? If so, you have some traces of society-centering in you. Such terms as real world, problem solving, democracy, and citizenship are favorites of those who are drawn to this curriculum model. This is an activist model of curriculum.

This is a curriculum based on social issues. The orientation is toward problems of living: life problems, community affairs, and real world problems. The curriculum, or at least the raw material for the curriculum, already exists in the real world. One does not need sterile textbooks, empty exercises, and never-ending seat work to distract us from the real work at hand, so the thinking goes. The issues are all around us in the local environment and beyond, waiting for teachers and students to get involved as a class or as a school. Figure 6.1 lists keys to the society-centered curriculum.

The foundation of the society-centered curriculum is built on real-world problems. Social issues are the content, not academic subject matter nor the child's individual growth and development. Saving a salmon stream, making the classroom or school a better place, and school-to-work experiences, are examples of society-centering. You will inevitably find in the society-centered curriculum the image of students and teachers as activists trying to escape the narrow confines of the classroom for the real world where real problems exist.

The renowned curriculum expert John Goodlad (1984) once observed that, ironically, students come to school to learn alone in groups. By this he meant that students are typically told to do their own work and to keep their eyes on their own papers while being surrounded by other students. This is not society-centering. After all, such an outlook is hardly conducive to making the classroom a miniature society, a community, a democracy. If the primary purpose of school is social education, the focus must be on group problem solving in the real world, working together, team building, collaborative effort, and cooperative learning as essential elements of school life.

Figure 6.1. Keys to the Society-Centered Curriculum

Emphasis	◆ Search for social relevance ◆ Education for citizenship
Teaching	◆ Problem-solving units ◆ Subject matter disciplines as tools ◆ Community resource people ◆ Team planning/Teach teaching/Team learning
Learning	◆ Group projects ◆ Cooperative efforts ◆ Leadership opportunities
Environment	◆ Classroom/school as democracy ◆ Cross-age/Cross-grade ◆ Real world as learning laboratory
Assessment	◆ Real world outcomes ◆ Citizenship and leadership development ◆ Applied knowledge and skills ◆ Group reflection ◆ Social growth

As we establish the keys to the society-centered curriculum, I want you to think about yourself and your own world view of teaching and learning. To what extent do you identify with these elements? The focus is on social activity. The school and therefore the curriculum are primarily socially engaged.

Participation is the key, participation especially in real world activity. Pageants, dramas, team projects, school assemblies, school government, co-operative learning, changing the environment for the better, ecology, preservation efforts, peace education, etc., are the essence of the curriculum. This is the day-to-day stuff of the society-centered curriculum. Relevance to the real world and leaving the world a better place than you found it through group efforts are the heart of the enterprise. Typically, this means projects in the community.

The project approach dominates the society-centered curriculum, particularly the group project approach as opposed to individual projects and efforts; at stake is the *esprit de corps* (the common spirit) that develops when people work together with a shared sense of purpose. In order to achieve this, the most valued form of learning and teaching in the society-centered curriculum is the class or group project. In the project approach, there is very little interest in or respect for the academic disciplines as separate subjects or as ends in themselves. The function of the academic disciplines is that of tools to help solve problems.

In this respect, subject matter does not represent an end in itself. For example, do students need to know a certain amount of mathematics, of science, English, etc., to solve a particular problem in the real world? If that's the case, and it usually is, then they use subject matter as a tool, just as a carpenter uses a hammer, not as an end in itself, but as a tool to do the job. As Beane (1997, p. 96) writes, "the primary use of knowledge in the curriculum ought to be in responding to significant self and social issues."

Well, you can see this raises certain problems with scope and sequence because one cannot prescribe the curriculum ahead of time as one might a knowledge-centered curriculum. If responding to social issues *is* the curriculum, this means taking up life problems, and we don't necessarily know what they're going to be. Real world problems tend to be messy and often unforeseen. For middle school students, it might be the experience of trying to figure out who they are as they come of age. To build a curriculum around such a topic requires adult guidance, to be sure, but it could hardly be meaningfully accomplished without significant student planning as well. The issues must come from the learners' life experiences. However, it is limiting to think only in terms of the learners' experience. A good teacher will help students to generalize their findings or to make more global applications.

Consider the case of an elementary class that might otherwise have been studying science in a traditional sense, learning from text with perhaps some hands-on experience thrown in, paper and pencil test to follow. Instead, we find the class outdoors working in a wildlife refuge to keep it ecologically clean, preserving the habitat, perhaps under the guidance of a park ranger. There is no denying the fact that these students need to read, to know some biology, ecology, mathematics, geography, etc. But the point is that they are trying to solve a set of problems in a meaningful context, so academic knowledge and skills are not ends in themselves, but useful tools for problem solving.

This vision of the curriculum and of school life is intriguing. The English word, "*school*" derives from the Greek word, "*schola,*" that in the days of Socrates, Plato, and Aristotle signified a place of leisure, a place set apart from the real world. It was purposely *not* the real world. The premise was that the real world is not a place of ideas. The real world is a place of activity. Ideas are the product of reflection, and for reflection to happen, a place must be set apart for it. Of course, such schools were for the select few.

Advocates of the society-centered curriculum, however, will inevitably argue that the best experiences the school can offer are real world experiences. This view of school propriety decries the artificial nature of textbooks and a curriculum carved up into separate subjects that have little or nothing to do with one another. The need is to engage the culture, to become involved in the community that lies beyond the school doors, to make a difference. Young people are at a formative, idealistic stage of life, and they need to learn that they can and should make a difference in the world. These arguments are for knowledge applied, for citizenship lived, for shared experience beyond the school walls.

Emphasis on the Group and the Self in Group Context

In the society-centered curriculum, the focus is on the group and on group action. The individual (and his/her growth and development) is considered in group context. The question is, "what can the group accomplish? What can we do together that we could not do individually?" In the learner-centered curriculum, obviously, the focus is on the individual, and in the knowledge-centered curriculum the focus is quite clearly on academics. These are oversimplifications, to be sure, but they point toward basic, underlying priorities. They help us come to terms with what is at stake if we follow this path versus that one.

Not all society-centered approaches to curriculum involve environmental projects. The school-to-work activities that have become popular in high schools are also an example of the society-centered curriculum. Students who think they might want to enter certain careers are given opportunities to spend time at hospitals, businesses, and other places of work as pan of their school experience. They are challenged to find out directly what is involved in the workplace and to take part in it. The whole career education movement, in the variety of forms it has taken over the years, is based on the society-centered model.

Society-centered curriculums are problem-solving curriculums. They focus on problems that engage the real world, rather than artificial problems, puzzles, exercises or activities found in textbooks. The society-centered teacher encourages the class to explore the local community to see what the problems are and see to what extent they could focus on those problems, and do something to make the our world a better place. If there's a nursing home in the area, the society-centered teacher is quite likely to encourage students to consider the plight of the elderly in our society, not merely as an abstract matter, but as a matter of involvement. Older people shut up in nursing homes often feel lonely and isolated and depressed. What can we do to improve the quality of their lives? How can we contribute? A project begins to take shape, an experience that will involve students in all the stages of problem solving from perceiving a need, defining the issues, planning, taking needed action, and reflecting on the degree of success of the effort.

The society-centered teacher is far more interested in creating conditions of democracy, participation and citizenship than in teaching academic knowledge as though it were valuable for its own sake. As Eby (1952, p. 659) noted long ago, "Only knowledge that functions is treasured and only for the time being." In fact, society-centered teachers tend to think of academic knowledge and the information found in traditional sources such as textbooks as inert knowledge, dead knowledge unless it functions, unless it is somehow applied. They view knowledge that comes from experience in the real world as knowledge that is alive, organic, real, and life changing.

Teacher Role

The teacher's role is that of facilitator in ways somewhat similar to that of the learner-centered curriculum. The difference is that here one finds a focus not so much on the individual but on facilitating group efforts, of getting kids to see that they are in this together, that they need each other, that you have to have a group to do this, whether it is putting on a play, a science fair, making the environment cleaner or the school safer, etc. While this may seem obvious, it is more of a challenge than one might imagine. Students should work in groups, of course. But more than one group-oriented teacher has learned the hard way the need for developing social skills, for creating a climate of collaboration, and for genuine team building.

One of the clichés that goes with the society-centered curriculum is "think globally and act locally." No doubt you have heard this before. However, there is something to it. A good example of such a society curriculum is that which came to light about a child living in southern Mexico who saw that the rainforest in her area was being depleted rapidly because of the growth of coffee plantations and related clear cutting for ranching and agriculture. And so, she began with her classmates to write to students around the world to see if they could put together a "team" using the Internet to begin to bring pressure to bear on people to stop despoiling local environments. Her focus was on her local environment, which happened to be a rainforest, but she was acting locally and thinking globally, getting others from around the world to become involved as well. Obviously, teachers can help to facilitate such efforts. These kinds of things typically don't happen without good teachers.

Another example comes from a teacher in Victoria, British Columbia, Canada, who got her middle school students involved in a crusade to stop the use of Styrofoam cups on the British Columbia ferry system. The students conducted scientific research to show why paper cups are better to use than Styrofoam cups, and what the effect on the environment is. Called on to present their findings, the students were persuasive in getting the B.C. ferry system to drop the use of Styrofoam containers and make a change to paper containers. It took a teacher to facilitate that. It took leadership on the part of the teacher to mobilize the kids to do what they're capable of doing.

Integrated Studies

You won't find a traditional subject matter curriculum in the society-centered environment. Rather, you find what are known as integrated studies. Integrated studies represent a type of curriculum in which the focus is on problems. With a problem focus, teachers and students work backward from the problem, asking how or whether the subject matter disciplines can be of help. What knowledge and skills are needed to write an effective letter to the city council? What do students need to know about basic science if they are going to gather useful soil and water samples? Knowledge functions as tools in a tool chest, used when needed. The point is that academic disciplines are means to be used to solve problems.

But there is more to integrated studies than using academic knowledge wisely. Social skills of group work, collaboration, and team building call for a more subtle integration: the integration of people. The argument that you cannot have moral education without social education becomes relevant. Because students are working together, they will find their own values put to the test. They will find themselves living with issues of justice, fairness, teamwork, collaboration, citizenship, democracy, caring, compassion, and a desire to improve conditions for everyone.

The question might well arise over a lack of attention in this book to critical theory and to neo-Marxist views of curriculum. The reasons I have not included this perspective is that it is basically nonexistent in American schools and it is primarily a critique of the way things are. It seldom takes the form of curriculum. Perhaps one of the most celebrated attempts was that made by Paulo Freiere, whose book, *Pedagogy of the Oppressed* (1970), created excitement in adult education circles in particular. Freiere's ideas of empowerment of the Brazilian poor through literacy programs brought about much acclaim. Freiere himself later became Minister of Education for Brazil, but it appears that he was more skilled as an outsider critiquing the obvious ills of educational systems in general than in making fundamental changes, given the inertia of the entrenched and the bureaucratic in the world of schools.

Summing Up

In a curriculum where subject matter and people are integrated, one reasonably expects to find a great deal of student-to-student interaction, decision-making and governance. This can be messy to the point that some teachers simply choose to avoid it. Working with others seems to come more naturally to some students than to others. But this is the essence of democracy. It is a reason why we have school. John Dewey referred to such growth opportunities that inevitably arise in collaborative efforts as collateral learning. Piaget called it social knowledge.

Always in a society-centered curriculum, there is a sense of reaching out to the community and getting outside the artificial constraints of the classroom. Both the learner-centered and society-centered curriculums come from progressive educational philosophy with all its emphasis on student interest, decision making, and active learning. They share much in common, especially a disdain for essentialist/traditionalist teaching and learning. Where they part company is over the matter of greater emphasis on the individual learner versus greater emphasis on the group and on the realization of private dreams versus making a difference in the world.

Your Turn

Before you read a personal account of a society-centered perspective and examine two exemplars, collect your own thoughts concerning two dispositions mentioned in the closing.

- ◆ How 'messy' is your ideal classroom?
- ◆ Do you have 'disdain' for any particular teaching practices?

The Principal Speaks:
A Society-Centered Curricular Perspective

Hal Sanders is principal of East Valley View Middle, a school with approximately 700 students in grades six through eight. He is a former classroom teacher and has been principal at East Valley for six years.

I never thought of myself as being society-centered or child-centered or whatever. But I do have a definite philosophy of education that I guess would make it seem that I am what might be called society-centered. I have a very clear idea of the central purpose of school. Think about it, these kids are important people, and their time is worth something. We don't want to waste it. We want to give them the best education we possibly can. So, when I ask myself, 'what is the purpose of school?' my answer is citizenship.

Of course, there are other reasons why young people should come to school, but in a democracy citizenship is the most important qualification. Citizenship as we have defined it in this society is a precious thing, and it brings with it a lot of responsibility as well as many rights and privileges. As much as we can, we run this school as a democracy. Students have power here, and that's the way we want it. So do they, for that matter. Sometimes I like to walk down the hall saying "Hello, Citizen Sasha!" or "Hello Citizen Jennifer!" They reply back to me, "Hello Citizen Sanders." And we really mean it.

Student government is a reality here. The students take elections very seriously, and they expect much of their elected leaders. A kid got elected student body president a couple of years ago by running on a platform where her campaign slogan was, "You're going to have to work hard if you elect me." Well, they did. She worked hard, too, setting an example. Our faculty really believes in participatory governance and full participation by every one. You see it in the academic curriculum as well as in the activity curriculum. We don't refer to the academic curriculum and the extra curriculum. It's all curriculum here.

You think this place is a bee hive during regular school hours. You ought to see it before regular hours and in the late afternoons. The average kid spends over seven hours a day here, and it's productive time that eats into things like after school television watching. We have just about any kind of club you can think of: chess club, language clubs, intramural teams, newspaper and magazine, international club, music club, art club, science club, explorers club, you name it, we've got it. Each club has a sponsor, and it turns out to be a great way for teachers and kids to get to know each other better.

I know it's a cliché, but 'relevance' is really a watchword here. Our entire faculty is always busy dreaming up ways to make the academic curriculum relevant to the outside world and to the world of the kids. You wouldn't maybe think that a course like Pre Algebra lends itself to community service, but it does here. Some of the connections are more obvious, like earth science and local conservation of the environment. I really think you could walk down the halls of East Valley talking to the kids you meet, and everyone of them could tell you about a service project they're involved in.

When you expect this much of the students you have to figure out ways to articulate things so that kids don't get overloaded. Our faculty works as a team and as groups of sub teams to make sure that homework, projects, other assignments, even club activities are understood by everyone. Of course, we involve the community as well. Our parking lot is always full because we encourage parent and community involvement. I think one of the reasons we can keep so much going on here is because of the tremendous volunteer effort we get from folks, many of whom don't even have kids at our school.

We keep the school open at least two nights a week for school and community hobbies, sports, art, music, theater, homework, library, mathematics, foreign language, chess tournaments, whatever. The community people know this school is here for them and they use it. I think this goes a long way toward deepening our students' sense of citizenship. They see adults giving their time and participating, and they think that's just naturally the way things are. We don't have a special open house night because the place is open on a regular basis.

I haven't said much about academics. We encourage team building, cooperative learning, support groups, anything we can do to build a sense of togetherness and community. I think our academic standards are high, but I'm certain one reason for that is that we do everything we can to make every student feel needed and welcome. For some kids, this comes naturally, but others who maybe are a little shy or afraid are made to feel such a part of the place that you just love the way they grow into the spirit of things.

I know every student by name, and when someone transfers in during the school year, I make it a point to have lunch with them and find out about their interests and their dreams. I like to visit classrooms every day just to lend support or to teach a lesson from time to time. So do our other two administrators. They're out there all the time; you can hardly find them in their offices. Our teachers and students are wonderful about making sure everyone is included as much as possible. We don't want anyone left behind when it comes to friendship.

This probably isn't a perfect place, but it sure is a friendly, caring place. But sitting here listening to me isn't enough. Let's go out and meet some citizens.

Your Turn

Both the teacher and the learner have been mentioned as components of the curriculum exemplars; this perspective was provided by the principal.

- ◆ What is the role of the administrator in your concept of the ideal school?

Exemplar 4

The Foxfire Curriculum

Cultural Journalism

Description and Brief History

The Foxfire curriculum began in 1966 in Appalachian Georgia as an attempt "to engage rural youth in relevant community-based experiences that would both develop their literacy skills and preserve local tradition" (Kugelmass 1995, p. 3). The Foxfire approach, developed by Eliot Wigginton, began as "an experiential education program originally intended to teach basic English skills to high school freshmen" through cultural journalism (Starnes 1999, p. 1). Wigginton's Foxfire project called for students to interview "community members who had expertise or historical perspectives and [write] about what they learned" (AASA, online p.1). At the heart of the Foxfire curriculum are the student-produced *Foxfire Magazine* and a series of books on Appalachian life.

Following Foxfire's national circulation, teachers adapted the Foxfire concept and, by 1979, 150 similar student publications had been created (Olmstead, 1989). By 1988, at least 109 schools continued to publish student-produced cultural journalism (Olmstead, 1989). The Foxfire curriculum is now recognized as the overall curriculum approach that emerged from those original cultural journalism publications and the accompanying classroom experiences (Starnes). The Foxfire approach is currently used by teachers in 38 states (AASA).

Philosophy

Starnes (1999) states that the Foxfire approach to teaching and learning is defined by eleven core practices that emerged from the original Foxfire project's classroom experiences. Foxfire's eleven core practices provide a framework for teaching, learning, and assessment practices:

1. Classroom work is infused with student choice and design.
2. The teacher's role is collaborator and facilitator.

Foxfire

3. The academic integrity of the work is clear.
4. The work is characterized by active learning.
5. Emphasis is placed on small-group work, peer teaching, and inclusion of all students.
6. Connections between class work and the community are clear.
7. There is an audience beyond the teacher for student work.
8. New learning includes previously acquired skills and understandings.
9. Learning experiences encourage creative thought and action;
10. Reflection occurs at key points throughout the work.
11. The work includes rigorous, ongoing assessment.

Starnes (1999) and her colleagues Paris and Stevens, explain Foxfire's eleven core practices in the following way:

1. The work teachers and learners do together is infused from the beginning with learner choice, design, and revision.
2. The role of the teacher is that of facilitator and collaborator.
3. The academic integrity of the work teachers and learners do together is clear.
4. The work is characterized by active learning.
5. Peer teaching, small-group work, and teamwork are all consistent features of classroom activities.
6. Connections between the classroom work, the surrounding communities, and the world beyond the community are clear.
7. There is an audience beyond the teacher for learner work.
8. New activities spiral gracefully out of the old, incorporating lessons learned from past experiences, building on skills and understandings that can now be amplified.
9. Imagination and creativity are encouraged in the completion of learning activities.
10. Reflection is an essential activity that takes place at key points throughout the work.
11. The work teachers and learners do together includes rigorous, ongoing assessment and evaluation.

Cultural Journalism as Curriculum

The Foxfire curriculum consists of cultural journalism. Olmstead (1989) states that although cultural journalism is not a new process, the term "was first used to describe publications inspired by" the Foxfire magazines (online p. 1). Olmstead (1989) states that, in cultural journalism, "authors chronicle the traditional skills and values of many different groups, defined perhaps by ethnic origin, occupation, or environment." (online p. 1). Student-produced cultural journalism publications take a variety of forms: books, magazines, newspapers, and anthologies.

Additionally, cultural journalism can take a variety of non-print forms: videos, audiotapes, radio broadcasts, television productions, and websites. Olmstead (1989) states that cultural journalism benefits students in that it "provides a practical, tangible reason for students to do academic work" (online p. 2). Because the end product is meant for public review, the students "take seriously the task of using language effectively and correctly" and the notion of academic integrity (Olmstead, 1989).

Teacher and Student Roles

The Foxfire approach, rather than delineating the roles of teacher and student, stresses the relationships among teachers, learners, curriculum, and community (Starnes 1999, online p.2). The Foxfire curriculum is "learner-centered and community focused" (Starnes, 1999, online p.2). The teacher serves to coordinate students' participation in the decisions that affect the learning objectives and the integration of the curriculum into the community. Teachers "help students identify ways they can learn required skills and content by seeking information and resources from within the community" (AASA). Students interact with their sources in the community and with each other with the common purpose of publishing a tangible product of cultural journalism.

Assessment

In the Foxfire approach, students are involved in their own assessment, and are expected to develop it as a natural part of their inquiry and learning. "Teachers are encouraged to involve students in developing performance evaluations to ensure that their activities are meeting curriculum expectations" (AASA, online p. 3). In other words, traditional assessment forms are not particularly relevant. Students conduct real world investigations, and the idea is that any assessment should reasonably flow from that, especially in the form of some write-up, display, or performance. The fact that Foxfire inquiry is done not as a mere academic activity, but for the purposes of publication in various forms, means that the meeting of deadlines, use of proper grammar, integrity in reporting, and the ability to communicate fluently and accurately to a reading public are the kinds of assessment rarely realized in school life.

Your Turn

♦ What do you make of the Foxfire curriculum model?

♦ What might make it a true composite of curriculum types? or What keeps it from being a true composite?

♦ Given that no curriculum will be completely devoid of any one of the three centers, what proportion of each would you say influences your thinking about classroom decisions? Separate the circle into sections depicting relative influence.

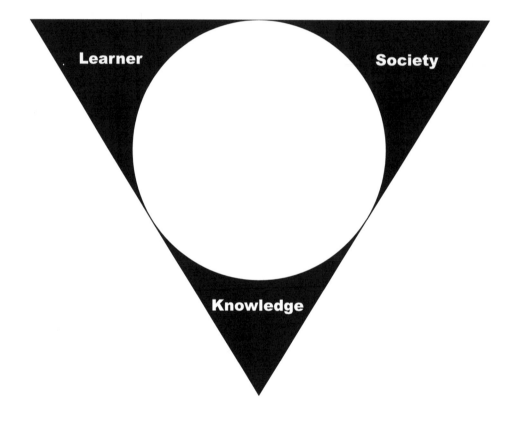

The Unified Science and Mathematics for Elementary Schools (USMES) Approach

Real World Problem Solving

The Unified Science and Mathematics for Elementary Schools (USMES) is funded by the National Science Foundation (NSF). The USMES curriculum project grew out of recommendations made by participants at the 1970 Cambridge Conference on the Correlation of Science and Mathematics in Schools. The idea of USMES is for teachers and students to identify and attempt to solve together real problems in their local environment.

The curriculum is comprised of more than twenty different challenges or problems to be solved, always with a focus on local issues at the classroom, school, or community level, such as those listed below. The problems or challenges are taken-up by a class as an integrated unit of study.

Exemplary USMES Unit Titles

- *Soft Drink Design*—The problem-solving challenge is to design a soft drink that has appeal to others. Students spend time developing formulas and working on cost analyses, nutrition, and advertising.

- *Manufacturing*—The challenge is for the class to come up with an idea for a product that is needed and that they can actually manufacture, market, and sell.

- *Consumer Research*—The challenge is to develop and carry out scientific tests that assess the value of various products, especially products that students themselves consume.

USMES

- *Finding Your Way*—The challenge is to investigate and map alternative ways (fastest, safest, most scenic) to get from one place to another in the local environment.

- *Weather Predictions*—The challenge is learn ways to predict the weather, especially for certain events (field day, class picnic, holidays, etc.) in which the students have some real reason for doing so.

- *Nature Trails*—The challenge is for the class to learn how nature trails are made and to actually construct one in the environment.

- *Eating at School*—The challenge is for the class to make recommendations for improving the nutritional, esthetic, and collegial atmosphere of the school lunchroom, etc.

- *Bicycle Transportation*—The challenge is for the class to investigate bicycle safety and to develop a plan for improving the general use of bicycles by students at and around the school.

- *Traffic Flow*—Students study traffic patterns in environment, including the school hallways, play areas, etc., and make recommendations for needed improvements.

As the acronym USMES implies, the students use mathematics and science skills and knowledge as tools to help them solve problems, but invariably the social sciences, language arts, and even music and art come into play. True to its progressive roots, USMES focuses on subject matter from the disciplines not as something necessarily intrinsically worthwhile, but as tools. In that respect, it satisfies the conditions of the progressive philosophy of instrumentalism.

The problem-solving challenges or units include such topics as "Manufacturing," in which a class is challenged to come up with an idea for a product, develop it, mass produce it, and sell it to consumers. The class often takes a small loan from a local bank to provide capital for the venture. Materials are purchased, tasks are divided up among the students, and issues such as quality control and pricing are carefully investigated along the way. The students learn such concepts as "profit and loss," "inventory," "scarcity," "division of labor," and "quality control."

A unit titled "Consumer Research" involves the testing of products that children regularly consume, such as breakfast cereal, peanut butter, school supplies, etc. Critical thinking comes into play as students study such advertising devices as endorsements by popular figures, techniques such as appeal to prestige, belonging or status, and economic value. Students often write letters or mount campaigns over defective or unsafe products, misleading claims, and general consumer satisfaction. In many ways, the conduct of the Consumer Research unit is reminiscent of the work done by such groups as

Public Interest Research Groups, Ralph Nader and his associates, and Consumer Reports. The unit is very much in the social activist tradition.

In any USMES unit, the focus is on the group's (not the individual's) attempt to solve a real problem. Typically, a unit lasts for three or four weeks, and more often than not, it provides a natural transition into another unit. USMES units are based on integrated studies, rather than on separate subjects, calling upon skills and knowledge from science, mathematics, language arts, social studies, and other areas of the school curriculum. However, such knowledge and skills represent tools for solving problems and are not studied as ends in themselves. So, for example, when students are testing certain products, they use their study of advertising methods, content analysis, and various measurement techniques to reach conclusions and make recommendations.

Student Role

The role of the teacher is crucial, but it clearly is that of facilitator rather than director of learning. The idea is that the students must take responsibility for deciding on appropriate investigatory methods, dividing up responsibilities, analyzing data, preparing reports, and making recommendations. The USMES approach frowns on independent study and isolated student learning. Always, the focus returns to the group, and each day a class meeting is scheduled for the purpose of reviewing progress, discussing difficulties, maintaining focus, making corrections, sharing insights, and assigning tasks. The teacher makes suggestions, provides any needed arbitration, and helps students with finding materials and sources, but his/her role is that of guide rather than director of learning.

One interesting feature of the USMES curriculum is the "skills session." Skills sessions are typically taught by the teacher, although sometimes by an outside expert or even by one or more of the students themselves. Skills sessions are typically didactic and are taught by demonstration or by direct instruction. They are designed to fit the idea of John Dewey's "teachable moment," a theory that states that "when students want or need to know something connected to their lives, the equation is changed from traditional out-of-context teaching to meeting a need." To take an example, it often becomes necessary for students to process data they are collecting, perhaps daily temperatures (in the Weather Predictions Unit) or tabulations from a survey of the student body (in the Eating at School Unit). In the case of the daily temperatures, the teacher may teach a skills session on how to construct a line graph, thereby enabling the students to graphically record and display the temperatures they have collected over time. In the case of the survey, the teacher may teach a skills session on how to select a random sample of the student body so that students do not have to interview every student in the school.

In the unit titled, "Pedestrian Crossings," students take up the problem of studying a crosswalk near the school. The unit presents a practical problem because almost any school has a crosswalk near it that poses potential dangers. A fifth grade class in St. Paul, Minnesota, studied a crosswalk at the school, making maps and models, interviewing younger students as well as neighborhood residents, timing the speed of cars, and studying city traffic laws. The class presented its findings in the form of written and oral reports to the City Council's traffic commission and was successful in bringing about several notable changes, including the posting of new signs, repainting of the crosswalk, and a promise that the police would strictly enforce the legal speed limit of 20 mph during school hours.

Implicit in the USMES approach, and clearly present in the unit experience just described, is John Dewey's idea of the school as a miniature democracy with real world connections. The students who investigated the crosswalk near their school became directly involved in the democratic process, exercising their rights and obligations as citizens to make their world a better place. The progressive argument is that such an experience is far more valuable and instructive than merely reading about democracy from a textbook because it represents the educationally significant difference between actual and vicarious experience.

A key ongoing feature of any USMES unit is the almost daily class meeting. Such meetings are necessary to ensure that the focus on the problem is maintained, that the entire class is involved, that problems (whether, social, tactical, or whatever) are discussed and dealt with fairly, and that the energy of the group is maintained. Without such meetings, USMES units often wear down with both teacher and students losing interest. The daily meetings underscore the idea of a classroom as a miniature democracy where students meet to engage the important issues of daily life.

Teacher Role

A key component of the USMES model is an energetic teacher who will support the 'messiness' of real problem solving by his/her students. The USMES curriculum demands much of the teacher. There are no pre-planned lessons, no script to follow, no daily guide with questions and answers. Because of the curriculum's connection to the outside world, teachers must contact resource people, arrange field trips, scrounge materials, and generally disrupt the orderly, quiet, "keep your eyes on your own paper and do your own work" nature of classroom teaching and learning. Experience has shown that when carefully nurtured units can be eminently worthwhile, the energy they demand argues for limiting the experience to perhaps one or two units per year.

USMES units are real-world problem solving experiences. Therefore, the units are fluid in nature, open to the dictates of local conditions, and largely unscripted. Emphasis is placed on group work with a whole-class focus on the central problem at hand, for example, "how can we make eating at school a more enjoyable experience?" Knowledge and skills from science, English, mathematics, social studies, and the arts are seen as tools for solving real-world problems. An integral part of the teacher's job is to ensure that the whole class remains focused on the challenge, that basic skills are integrated into the problem-solving efforts, and to facilitate group work and student efficacy.

Assessment

USMES, in true progressive tradition, does not advocate formal testing of students. Rather, the assessment is authentic in that students are themselves to evaluate the effects of their efforts. For example, in the Pedestrian Crossings Unit, they were able to make a significant change by convincing the traffic commission to place better warning signs, highlight the crosswalk near the school, etc. In the Manufacturing Unit, students assess everything from the success of the sales of the goods they manufactured, to the quality control, and even to the extent that every one in class became meaningfully involved. Needless to say, much of the meaningful gains in any society-centered unit are considered from the standpoint of community involvement on the part of the students, citizenship education, and the experience of working together to bring about positive change in the real world.

The crucial matter of assessment inevitably arises. What exactly do students learn from such experiences, particularly with reference to basic knowledge and skills? Critics point to a lack of systematic exposure to knowledge and skills that students receive from a prescribed scope and sequence. The matter is hardly trivial, and no doubt certain basic knowledge and skills are missed under certain circumstances. However, in a study of economic knowledge, skills, and concepts (Ellis and Glenn, 1980), a class of randomly-assigned students who took up the month-long challenge of Manufacturing (they manufactured and sold school folders), outperformed their randomly-assigned counterparts who received daily instruction in economics using a teacher-directed workbook approach. The USMES group achieved a statistically significant higher mean score on a nationally-normed test of economic understanding developed by the Joint Council on Economic Education. Of course, this was one study, and not too much should be made of it. Still, the empirical evidence did favor the progressive problem-solving experience. Further, when presented individually with a new problem and asked to write about how they would go about solving it, the USMES students statistically outperformed the direct instruction class on measures of fluency and flexibility, which are crucial to problem-solving ability.

Perhaps the greatest strengths of the USMES curriculum are its emphasis on whole-class problem solving, where every student takes part in the venture, its emphasis on solving real-world problems that young people care about, and its emphasis on democracy and citizenship with the clear understanding that to solve real world problems one must participate in the commonweal. In addition to these benefits of the USMES approach, there are those of important skills taught in context at teachable moments, the active, hands-on constructive nature of learning that invariably occurs, and the sense of responsibility that students must take on to do the work since so much of it is student planned, initiated, and carried out.

Your Turn

The purpose of the USMES curriculum is to involve students in group projects in which students come up with real solutions to real problems. Troubleshoot this for your own classroom.

- How would this benefit the children you personally know?
- What would be the obstacles to implementing this?

7

The Knowledge-Centered Curriculum

...the term "academic curriculum" does not refer to the formalistic methods, role recitations, and student passivity about which all reasonable educators and parents have justly complained. Nor does it refer only to teaching skills. It refers instead to the systematic study of language and literature, science and mathematics, history, the arts, and foreign languages; these studies, commonly described today as a "liberal education," convey important knowledge and skills, cultivate aesthetic imagination, and teach students to think critically and reflectively about the world in which they live.

Diane Ravitch

The best education for the best is the best education for all.

Mortimer Adler

Welcome to the knowledge-centered curriculum, also known as the academic curriculum. Please note the quote above written by educational historian and former U.S. Undersecretary of Education Diane Ravitch, reminding us that this approach to the curriculum stresses academic rigor, but not necessarily at the expense of innovative methods. This chapter introduces several variations on the knowledge-centered curriculum. As you read about them, consider them reflectively and try to imagine how your school would change if you adopted one of these approaches or perhaps some combination of them.

Let us begin with the goal structure. It is pretty straightforward in one sense: to learn the canon. But what is meant by that? The canon represents the agreed upon essential knowledge that students should learn. Advocates of the knowledge-centered curriculum make it clear that what students are to receive is a liberal education, meaning an academic education: no vocational track, no practical math, no life skills courses, etc. If indeed students are to acquire a liberal education, the source of which is the canon, or the agreed upon academic curriculum, what, then will they study? This is where things become a little messy.

There probably was a time in American school history when considerable agreement over the academic course of study existed. This is no longer the case for three rather different reasons: the increasingly pluralistic nature of society, the knowledge explosion, and effort in recent years to send everyone to school.

It is difficult for anyone who does not remember times of racial segregation and the exclusion of women from leadership positions to comprehend just how much society has changed in the course of a generation or two. American society has achieved levels of equality of opportunity that would have been seen as unattainable by past standards. The children's card game, *Authors*, provides us with some minor insight to the way things were. The game, which is still available but not nearly so popular as it was, utilized a deck of famous authors who basically represented the canon of school literature: Shakespeare, Dickens, Longfellow, Hawthorne, etc. They were British and American, and with the exception of Louisa May Alcott, male authors. The literature curriculum of the past was pretty much like the card game: women authors were under-represented and rarely to be found, and authors of color were absent from the list.

Second, the knowledge explosion is a very real thing. There are more authors, scientists, and investigators of all kinds today. Scientific knowledge has expanded exponentially. Today, there simply is more mathematics, literature, science, and history than there was. Consider what we know today about health and nutrition compared to what we knew a generation ago. The academic subjects in the curriculum derive from scholarly disciplines where researchers daily make new discoveries, enlarging the knowledge base. What to leave in and what to leave out of a history or a science textbook is not an easy thing to decide. So, the task of getting agreement on what constitutes the most important knowledge, skills, and values is considerably harder than it used to be.

And third, arguments inevitably arise over whether the academic course of study, regardless of its merit for some, is suited to all students' needs. There are those who argue that the academic or knowledge-centered curriculum should be reserved for those students who clearly will go on to pursue a university education, while students of lesser academic ability should take vocational and practical courses. A century ago, when ten to fifteen percent of students completed high school, it was far easier to expect high academic standards. Today, when virtually all students participate in secondary education, such a curriculum seems elitist at best and largely irrelevant. It is not unusual for secondary teachers to say that the wide range of academic ability, level of motivation to learn, and interest or lack of interest in subject matter found in a typical high school class makes it extremely difficult to teach academic subjects effectively.

On the surface these issues alone would seem to argue against attempts to put together a meaningful knowledge-centered curriculum, given the numbers of students enrolled in schools today. Far better, critics say, to abandon the separate subject matter approach and to embrace either a curriculum of direct social relevance or of self-realization. But as we will see, advocates of knowledge-centered approaches to the curriculum argue that theirs is the truly democratic, opportunity-based curriculum.

A Liberal Education

As we have seen, the learner-centered curriculum sets forth the noble goal of self-realization or the self-actualization of the individual's dreams and aspirations in life. In other words, it is self-centered, although such a description is easily open to misinterpretation and caricature. The purpose of school from this perspective is to facilitate the needs and desires of the learner, to enable him/her to become a fulfilled individual. Most of us would agree that this is important and that the school should do what it can to make this possible.

However, we can as well admit that there may be other reasons for coming to school, even other avenues than a curriculum based on learner interest, for achieving self- realization. In the case of the knowledge-centered curriculum, a sense of purpose derives from a vision of the well-educated person. School, the argument goes, should equip learners with a liberal education, that is, a broad knowledge of science, literature, history, mathematics, and the arts; furthermore, there is no way to do this short of a rigorous academic course of study. The fundamental premise is that knowledge is an end in itself, particularly knowledge of the best themes of literature, the beauty and symmetry of mathematics, the perspectives of history, the wonders of science, and the uplifting nature of the arts.

A supporting argument is that the well-educated person is invariably the most adaptable, the most prepared for the unknown, the best citizen. This is so because knowledge of academics has a civilizing effect on human beings, so the argument goes. Such knowledge makes a person more rational, more reflective, and less inclined to impulsive behaviors. An educated person is one who appreciates the finer things in life, including the arts, culture, heritage, and noble traditions. Those who disagree with this position typically have little more than its advocates have in the way of empirical proof of the clear and definite superiority of one of the educational views explained in this book over another.

The knowledge-centered curriculum typically does not allow for vocational courses. Advocates will say that a liberal education is the best preparation for the world of work because literate individuals make the best-prepared workers in a democratic society. The argument advanced by knowledge-centered curriculum enthusiasts is that vocational training for those who wish to pursue it should come after a student has completed his/her K–12 school experience. The point is that there is no argument over the value of vocational training; the argument is that it does not belong in the K–12 curriculum. Students who are well prepared academically should be in the best position to elect university, technical, or some other form of post-high school education.

The foundation of the knowledge-centered curriculum is subject matter from the academic disciplines. More often than not, courses emphasize separate subject matter or separate disciplines, although interdisciplinary approaches are sometimes advocated, especially in the early school years. But as students deepen their knowledge through what Ravitch (2000) and others call "systematic study," it becomes increasingly necessary to offer courses taught by expert teachers who are themselves students of their disciplines. Therefore, the most logical approach to the curriculum is to separate it into courses in biology, geometry, literature, history, and fine arts, to name a few. Separate courses demand scholar-teachers who themselves have spent years preparing and studying their subject matter. In one sense, however, there is no argument with an interdisciplinary curriculum as long as those who offer it are well prepared in the subjects represented.

While the separate subjects approach is more or less taken for granted at secondary levels, arguments rage over whether this is appropriate at elementary levels. In this regard, it is worth noting that the National Council of Teachers of Mathematics (NCTM) is clearly on record as recommending that beginning no later than fourth grade, mathematics should be taught to students by subject matter specialists. If the case can be made for mathematics, then why should geography not be taught by specialists? Why not literature? We know, for example, that many elementary teachers are frankly willing to admit that they are not particularly knowledgeable when it comes to teaching such subjects as science, mathematics, and history, particularly with doing much more than assigning the textbook and involving students in activities. It is only fair to say that few knowledge-centered critics of progressive education have called for special- subject teachers at pre-school or even primary levels. However, the old saying, "we teach children, not subjects," is hardly viewed as credible beyond the early years among knowledge-centered curriculum proponents.

Textbooks as Curriculum

Perhaps the best known, most widespread example of the knowledge-centered curriculum is the traditional course of study, governed mainly by textbooks. You are no doubt familiar with this approach because the chances are good you attended schools where the curriculum was organized by subject matter and controlled by textbooks. Curiously, even at primary levels one often finds a de facto separate subjects approach to the curriculum: reading from 9:00 to 10:00 A.M., mathematics at 11:00 A.M., etc., with textbooks or workbooks for each subject. And as students progress through the grades, they not only study separate subjects, they encounter different teachers, specialists, to teach those subjects. In other words, the curriculum is constructed not out of expressed learner interest, but out of academic knowledge derived from scholarly disciplines with accommodations made for childhood and adolescent capabilities. It is a familiar model to most of us. We could call it the business-as-usual approach for want of a better term. But before we dismiss this approach and move on, we should take a moment to consider the textbook as curriculum.

In conversation with a group of consultants to a National Science Foundation project, in which we were asking ourselves, "what is the best way to determine the nature of the curriculum in any particular subject" One of the more compelling responses was that the textbook is probably the single most explicit artifact of curriculum in American schools. Following this line of reasoning, if you wished to determine the curriculum being studied by a certain student, it would make sense for you to examine the textbooks the students are required to study.

Textbooks have their strengths. At least quite a few people seem to think so given the big business they represent and their ubiquitous presence in American public schools. Textbooks provide structure in the form of scope and sequence. They represent organized bodies of knowledge, collected between the covers of a single volume, that provide students with a basis for understanding a particular subject in ways that would take years for teachers to assemble, assuming they had the time. They also provide the "expert" knowledge that the teacher may not have. Teachers often must teach several subjects, and they have little time to prepare adequately. Even teachers who claim a certain amount of expertise in a particular subject may not know, or know well, some of the material a text covers. Textbooks ensure equal access to knowledge, providing each student with the basic information he/she needs. Teacher editions provide course objectives, teaching tips, suggested activities, questions to ask, exercises, and exams designed to flesh out and otherwise account for the material covered in the text.

Of course, many criticisms have been leveled at the textbook-dominated curriculum. Among those criticisms are:

- Textbooks are mostly commercial products produced by a near monopoly of three or four leading companies;
- they contain biased coverage of certain topics;
- they are often filled with factual errors;
- they are mostly dull and uninspiring;
- they contain little more than information and exercises with almost no problem solving, inquiry, or other opportunities for higher level thinking;
- they are basically a management tool more than anything else (as in "take out your textbook and turn to page 59...");
- they diminish teacher/student initiative and create a dependency cycle on a single source of information;
- they often have little correspondence to state standards and/or standardized tests, creating havoc with attempts to account for student learning to the general public;
- different published textbooks in a given subject often cover considerably different material, meaning that not as much consensus exists regarding what to leave in and what to leave out of the course of study as we might imagine.

One could go on, but no doubt the reader has the idea.

The fact remains that textbooks, from the ubiquitous basal readers found in nearly every primary classroom, to the science, mathematics, history, and English books that help to regulate the secondary course of study, are a mainstay of the knowledge-centered curriculum. The criticisms are obvious, but the adoptions continue. Seemingly, our American schools are addicted to textbooks. In an episode of the cartoon program, *The Simpsons*, the teacher textbook guides turned up missing at Springfield Elementary school, having the effect of shutting down the curriculum until they were later recovered. It was a playful spoof, but fully freighted with underlying truthful insight.

Curriculum as Process

As deeply ingrained as the textbook approach is to curriculum, however, not everyone in the knowledge-centered camp agrees that it is appropriate. Jerome Bruner, a cognitive psychologist who some years ago developed an experimental knowledge-centered curriculum called *Man: A Course of Study* (see Fig. 7.8), argued persuasively that the knowledge-centered curriculum is distorted when students merely study the formal outcomes or products of subject matter.

Figure 7.1. Jerome Bruner's Approach to Curriculum and Instruction

Bruner's Key Curriculum Concepts

- Structure
- Readiness
- Motivation
- Intuition

Bruner's Instructional Model

Enactive Learning:	with hands-on experience
Iconic Learning:	with imagery
Symbolic Learning:	with abstract ideas

Man: A Course of Study

What is human about human beings?

- Tool making
- Social organization
- Culturally-learned language
- Prolonged child rearing
- Worldview

How did human beings become human?

- Enculturation
- Evolution

How can human beings become more human?

In his experimental curriculum, students had access to primary source materials in the form of stories, film footage, and journals. They were required to become inquirers through activities, investigations, simulations, and a host of engaging learning strategies. Bruner's argument was that curriculum materials must be appealing, inviting, and otherwise capable of empowering the student as active learner.

Two of Bruner's books, *The Process of Education* (1960) and *The Culture of Education* (1996), are particularly stimulating reading for those interested in the annals of curriculum development. His emphasis on the process of education reminds us that students spend most of their school years studying the "tailings" of knowledge. They should instead, he maintained, study and experience the structure of knowledge. Basically, this means an inquiry/discovery approach focused on processes and concepts rather than on the products of science, mathematics, history, and other subjects. In Bruner's approach to the curriculum, students actually become historians, artists, mathematicians, and writers. This technique, called the structure of the disciplines approach, will be revisited later in the chapter.

Ways of Knowing

An intriguing approach to thinking about the curriculum is the *Ways of Knowing* model. This is knowledge centered, as the term implies. But it is a knowledge-centered approach with a difference. An apparently obscure book, found in most university libraries, is the place to start the quest. That book is the 84th yearbook of the National Society for the Study of Education (NSSE). In this yearbook edited by Elliot Eisner (1984), a number of distinctly different ways of knowing are presented. The book's message is that an alternative way to approach the knowledge-centered curriculum is to build a course of study around scientific ways of knowing, spiritual ways of knowing, narrative ways of knowing, mathematical ways of knowing, aesthetic ways of knowing, etc.

Knowledge can be organized by subject matter (geometry, biology, etc.), but that is not the only option. In the case of Ways of Knowing, teachers and students approach subject matter from truly different perspectives depending not only on the subject, but on the perspective the individual or group wishes to take on the subject. For example, the artistic perspective may well vary from the scientific perspective, and this is an important thing for young people to learn, because each perspective represents a different avenue for seeking truth. The storyteller certainly has a different task from that of the mathematician, but an awareness of both enables a person to think and act from more than one perspective. And the ability to blend the perspectives, for example, considering mathematics from a storytelling perspective, is further enriching.

It is unfortunate that Ways of Knowing has not become more prominent as a viable knowledge-centered approach to the curriculum. In some respects, it is related to Howard Gardner's far better known multiple intelligences theory. Ways of Knowing seems poised and waiting in the wings to bring a fresh set of insights to the meaning of knowledge centering. The emphasis on the role of perspective is empowering because it situates the learner as artist, scientist, or mathematician, as producer so to say, rather than merely as consumer. That school subjects might be considered from narrative, aesthetic, scientific, or spiritual perspectives (or any combination of these) seems to invite teachers and students to become members of the guild, partners with artists, historians, etc. In this respect, Ways of Knowing has the potential to bridge the all-too-real gap between learner-centered and knowledge-centered approaches because it accommodates in-depth interest with the rigor of knowing a discipline.

E. D. Hirsch's Core Knowledge Curriculum: Cultural Literacy

Yet another example of knowledge-centered curriculum is based on the idea of cultural literacy and known as the Core Knowledge Curriculum, developed by E. D. Hirsch, Jr. (1987), an emeritus professor of English at the University of Virginia. Hirsch's thesis is that you make *knowledge* (not concepts or skills) the goal of the curriculum. Given the other curriculums that are out there, this is actually a radical idea. You may have encountered the Core Knowledge Curriculum. It hasn't exactly swept the country, but it has found a definite niche in the K–8 curriculum pantheon. Hirsch, dissatisfied with the seeming ignorance of Americans, even those who had been "successful" in school, set out some years ago to argue the point that there is a commonly-held core body of knowledge that teachers should teach and students should learn as a result of the school experience.

The operative term is *knowledge*. An examination of the Core Knowledge Curriculum makes it perfectly clear that teachers and students are required to study literary classics, rules of grammar, fundamentals of mathematics, science, the arts, geography, and history. Those interested in learning more about Hirsch's knowledge-centered curriculum ideas will find his book, *The Schools We Need and Why We Don't Have Them* (1999), a useful place to start. One way to think of Hirsch's model is that it focuses on what he considers to be essential learnings. By essential learnings is meant the knowledge that Americans must possess in common if we are to have a culturally literate society. (This curriculum will be discussed in depth later in this chapter).

Mortimer Adler's *Paideia Proposal:*
An Educational Manifesto

It serves our purposes to note one other serious attempt at a knowledge-centered curriculum: the Paideia curriculum or the Paideia Proposal set forth by the late philosopher Mortimer Adler. Paideia is a Greek word that connotes the proper upbringing of a child. His book by that name, *The Paideia Proposal* (1982), generated considerable controversy when it was published more than two decades ago. The book is subtitled, *An Educational Manifesto*, so one imagines Adler knew that controversy would follow in its wake. It is interesting that Adler dedicated the book to Horace Mann, John Dewey, and Robert Hutchins. Mann to a certain extent and Dewey to a considerable extent are often claimed by advocates of progressive education, while Hutchins is firmly in the conservative, perennialist educational tradition.

Adler was motivated to write the book and indeed to take the leadership in the development of a curriculum because of his dismay over the "decline in the quality of public schooling." Among Adler's concerns were the amount of time teachers have to spend keeping order in classrooms at the expense of teaching and learning, the erosion of our democracy in which a declining proportion of the people vote or even attempt to be involved in the commonweal, the deleterious effects on workplace productivity as a result of poor schooling practices, and the ever-widening gap between the better and poorly educated.

The Paideia curriculum, according to Adler, is a curriculum founded in knowledge, to be sure, but not just information. Rather the curriculum focuses on knowledge of the great ideas that have occurred to profound thinkers throughout history: the knowledge of ideas such as duty, courage, honor, justice, freedom, citizenship, responsibility, and democracy, just to name a few. Adler's curricular ideas are rooted in an educational philosophy known as perennialism, since great ideas (for example, truth, justice, duty, democracy) are perennial, not temporary (see Fig. 7.2).

Figure 7.2. The Great Ideas (Hutchins, 1952)

Angel	Hypothesis	Poetry
Animal	Idea	Principle
Aristocracy	Immortality	Progress
Art	Induction	Prophecy
Astronomy	Infinity	Prudence
Beauty	Judgment	Punishment
Being	Justice	Quality
Cause	Knowledge	Quantity
Chance	Labor	Reasoning
Change	Language	Relation
Citizen	Law	Religion
Constitution	Liberty	Revolution
Courage	Life & death	Rhetoric
Custom & convention	Logic	Same & other
Definition	Love	Science
Democracy	Man	Sense
Desire	Mathematics	Sign & symbol
Dialectic	Matter	Sin
Duty	Mechanics	Slavery
Education	Medicine	Soul
Element	Memory & imagination	Space
Emotion	Metaphysics	State
Eternity	Mind	Temperance
Evolution	Monarchy	Theology
Experience	Nature	Time
Family fate	Necessity & contingency	Truth
Form	Oligarchy	Tyranny
God	One & many	Universal & particular
Good & evil	Opinion	Virtue & vice
Government	Opposition	War & peace
Habit	Philosophy	Wealth
Happiness	Physics	Will
History	Pleasure & pain	Wisdom
Honor		World

Adler believed that only the study of great ideas is educationally significant because ideas alone have the power to change the world. This approach stands in contrast to Hirsch's (1987, 1999) more essentialist philosophy that prepares for the world as it is.

Adler's theory of a curriculum based on great and perennial ideas represents yet another way to organize a knowledge-centered curriculum. An intriguing and controversial aspect of Adler's curriculum is that all students should receive the *same* course of study, no tracking, no vocational courses, strictly an academic curriculum. Aything less is in fact elitist and destructive of democracy, he argued. It is wrong to give students much choice over the curriculum because they are not sufficiently mature to truly know what they need to know in life. His vision was true to the knowledge-centered philosophy of adult control and supervision of the curriculum. The one concession he does make is to student choice of foreign language at secondary levels.

Of Differences and Similarities

You can see that general agreement exists among advocates of the knowledge-centered curriculum that a rigorous and challenging curriculum based on knowledge from the scholarly disciplines is the key. Still, there are certainly some real differences among knowledge-centered approaches. These differences broaden the choices available to those who are drawn to the basic idea. But keep in mind that in the knowledge-centered curriculum, however it is conceived, the orientation is always one of academic learning at the center.

Keys to the Knowledge-Centered Curriculum

Now, let us consider the keys to the knowledge-centered curriculum. In thinking about these keys, please ask yourself, "to what extent am I knowledge-centered versus learner-centered or society-centered? To what extent do I identify or disagree with each of these approaches? Are there some thoughtful ways of combining them?" Or are they so philosophically different that no meaningful accommodation could ever be achieved?

The first key to any knowledge-centered curriculum is a clear focus on acquiring the essential knowledge that constitutes a liberal education. It is a process that begins at the primary level and continues through high school graduation. Perhaps this seems obvious, but it is crucial to remind you of the progressive perspective that the primary purpose of school is social and that academic concerns, while important, are secondary. Such a difference in perspective is hardly trivial.

Whether through textbooks or other sources and means of gaining knowledge, the focus is always on academics. This leads us to a closely related key: the intellectual growth of the learner. A good knowledge-centered curriculum focuses on intellectual growth and development, on challenging the learner to go deeper into history, literature, mathematics, the arts, and other subjects. This is the point made by Diane Ravitch in the opening-of-chapter quote when she informs us that "formalistic methods" need not be part and parcel of the knowledge-centered curriculum. What is important, she writes, is that the "systematic study" of subject matter ought to be the reason students should come to school.

Yet another key to the knowledge-centered curriculum has to do with the nature of knowledge itself. What does it mean to know something? When is someone knowledgeable about a subject? Such questions lead inevitably to matters of assessment. In a truly learner-centered curriculum, assessment is mainly self-assessment. In a society-centered curriculum, assessment focuses on social relevance and real-world change. In the knowledge-centered curriculum, assessment more typically takes the form of standardized tests, of achievement tests, of ways of measuring what students know.

Knowledge is both product (knowing what) and process (knowing how), but learning must be measured or tested in some way. Testing often takes the form of multiple-choice standardized tests, but not necessarily so. Emphasis can as well be placed on essays and papers where students have the opportunity to express themselves without having to respond to closed-end questions; on oral examinations where students are asked questions and must think on their feet, giving the teacher a sense not merely of what they know, but of how they can use knowledge; or on performance, especially in the arts and sciences.

Even among those who agree that a knowledge-centered curriculum is best for students, there is a certain amount of controversy over the business of process versus product. Bruner has argued for emphasis on knowledge as process, and Hirsch for knowledge as product. Such matters are rarely as simple as they first appear, and Bruner and Hirsch would agree that both are necessary. However, most knowledge-centered curriculums are based on the assumption that knowing what is the place to begin. Hirsch's article, "You Can Always Look It Up—Or Can You?" (2001), addresses this very issue.

As a cognitive psychologist, Bruner has long argued that how we acquire knowledge is as important as the knowledge itself. Ravitch would agree as her chapter-opening quote attests. Therefore it is a serious misconception to think that one would encounter nothing more than teacher lecture, textbook presentation, and passive student learning in a knowledge-centered curriculum. In fact a great deal of emphasis can and should be placed upon performance, inquiry, and discovery, but always with the notion of building up knowledge. Almost no one denies that the process of coming to know is itself important. Bruner, far more passionately than, say Hirsch or Adler, argues that knowledge discovered (the process approach) is more powerful than knowledge gained from lecture or presentation because, he reasoned, knowledge discovered is knowledge owned whereas knowledge from other sources does not involve ownership on the part of the learner. The search for curricular balance, in this case between process and product, is never easy, and it remains one of the great challenges to any teacher no matter how the curriculum is designed.

Certainly in a knowledge-centered curriculum there is a focus on academic achievement. This very focus leads to questions about how well teachers themselves are prepared to teach a knowledge-centered curriculum. An argument often brought to bear by those who scorn the child-centered curriculum is that the real reason teachers object to knowledge-centering is that they themselves don't know much. It is axiomatic in knowledge-centering that the teacher is an achiever, a scholar who knows his/her material and who remains eager to learn, a model for children and adolescents (see Fig. 7.3).

One could reasonably ask the reading teacher, "What books have you read lately?"

One might ask the school principal, "To what extent are you a model of scholarship for your faculty and students?"

Figure 7.3. Keys To the Knowledge-Centered Curriculum

Emphasis	◆ Subject matter from academic disciplines ◆ Organized scope and sequence
Teaching	◆ Teacher as scholar/learner ◆ Teacher-directed curriculum ◆ Variety of teaching strategies
Learning	◆ Mastery of subject matter ◆ Student as novice learner
Environment	◆ Clear academic focus ◆ Traditional discipline ◆ School as workplace
Assessment	◆ Formal examinations ◆ Standards-based assessment

I mentioned earlier that the NCTM has recommended for many years that beginning with fourth grade, mathematics be taught by specialists in mathematics. Of course, learner-centered curriculum advocates typically do not agree, citing the importance of a deep relationship between teacher and students as more important than subject matter knowledge. And how, they argue, can meaningful relationships be achieved unless the student stays with one nurturing teacher rather than traipsing from room to room to receive instruction from so-called specialists? Progressives will say they teach the "whole child." Knowledge-centered advocates will say that is the problem, playing parent/counselor when they should be teaching academics.

Certainly, in a knowledge-centered classroom there is much less emphasis on the idea of the teacher as facilitator/nurturer than on the notion of the teacher as scholarly role model. A knowledge-centered curriculum demands scholar-teachers who know their subject matter inside and out. That doesn't guarantee that such persons are going to be good teachers; it merely happens to be a prerequisite. Without deep knowledge of subject matter, it is very difficult to lead students to deeper levels of understanding, so the argument goes.

In any curriculum, there is the matter of curriculum planning. Who should plan the curriculum? Let us explore certain points of contrast between the knowledge-centered curriculum and other approaches. In a learner-centered curriculum, as much of the curriculum as is possible is actually planned by the learner him/herself, based on interest. Such student planning is done in concert with the teacher, but nevertheless, the learner is a true policy-maker in planning the curriculum. Planning is largely individualized, so that in fact there are many curriculums at once in a given classroom. In a society-centered curriculum, we find the group, teacher and students, planning collectively. Knowledge-centered advocates uniformly agree that children should not plan their own curriculum. They argue that children and adolescents simply do not possess the maturity to know what is in their best interest for the long-term. Adler's and Hutchins' thinking that "the best curriculum for the best is the best curriculum for all," sums up the knowledge-centered perspective on this matter. It means that students will study a curriculum put together not by them but for them by caring adults.

A fixed idea, a recurring theme, of the knowledge-centered curriculum, is that there is a wisdom that teachers and other experts possess, that children simply do not have. One essentialist argument runs, "who would want undergraduates developing and determining the university curriculum?" If university undergraduates need a curriculum prepared and to a great extent selected for them, how much more do children need such adult guidance? Even when university students decide on a particular major course of study, they still do not plan or develop the courses themselves. Given the fact that we have, by all accounts, the best university system in the world, why would we want to change the curriculum by turning it over to the students?

The traditions and knowledge developed by scholars should shape the curriculum. The scope and sequence ought to be carefully and expertly designed from simple to more complex over time; this is what is meant by systematic study. But it is not the task of the learners to decide whether or not they want to study Shakespeare, to learn to read, or to study algebra; rather, this is a task for adults who have greater wisdom and knowledge of what students need to know now and in the future. And therefore, the scope and sequence of a knowledge-centered curriculum is carefully preplanned. This is not to say that there aren't choices for students to make within the curriculum. It is not unusual for teachers to encourage students to read different library books related to a particular topic of study, or to allow choice of projects or term papers, or even whether to have students work independently on topics of their own choosing, or in groups from time to time. Often there is room for choices within the structure or framework, but the framework of academic learning is definitely planned by people of greater age and experience than the learners.

The quest is to become an educated person. Often this quest is measured for better or worse by such academic outcomes as grades, test scores, and other means of sorting students. These inevitably become significant educational markers. SAT results and the results of other tests are used by colleges and universities to decide who gets in and who gets left out. Particularly as students in a knowledge-centered curriculum or school progress through the grades, they are made increasingly aware that their schoolwork represents preparation for university studies. A knowledge-centered curriculum that claims to be anything other than a college preparatory program at secondary levels is indeed hard to find. However, knowledge-centered advocates will often argue that even for the student who is not university bound, this represents the best preparation for life in general.

Knowledge-centered advocates argue that a well-educated person is simply more capable of enjoying the good life regardless of whether he/she goes on to university. They claim that liberally educated people make the best, most adaptable workers, the most informed citizens. To the primary teacher thinking ahead to the last years of schooling, it may be tempting to think that academic rigor is the province of the high schools. But the foundations of academic excellence are set in the early years, so the argument that knowledge-centering ought to be postponed until secondary school is unacceptable.

Traditional Curriculum Philosophies: Essentialism and Perennialism

Terms such as "back to basics" or "great ideas" are shortcuts or code for thinking about priorities in the school curriculum. If a curriculum is dedicated to getting back to the basics, then we can be sure that the guiding philosophy is that of essentialism. Essentialism is a philosophy of curriculum that means teaching and learning those things that are essential to success in life. If a curriculum is dedicated to great and unchanging ideas, then we can be sure that the guiding philosophy is that of perennialism. Perennialism is a philosophy of curriculum that means teaching and learning those great and enduring values that all serious thinkers have concluded are the essence of the good life.

American educational history offers insights to the development of these philosophies in our country. In Colonial times and well into the 19th Century, the Latin Grammar School offered a perennialist curriculum to the favored few. The Latin Grammar School as exemplified by the famous Boston Latin Grammar School, was a preparatory school for those few bound for higher education. The curriculum was rooted in history and the humanities, with heavy emphasis on such ancient languages as Latin, Greek, and Hebrew. The Latin Grammar Schools were purely academic, and were in that sense easily equal to a rigorous university education today.

In 1749, Benjamin Franklin, frustrated by the emphasis on a purely academic curriculum, founded Franklin's Academy in Philadelphia. The Academy also offered a rigorous academic curriculum, but it focused on those areas of learning that Franklin thought were essential to the building of a new nation. His curriculum offered navigation, engineering, surveying, and applied mathematics. This early form of essentialism set the tone for academies that rose up as challengers to the perennialist Latin Grammar Schools. Both continued to flourish through the 19th Century, gradually giving way, except for a number of private schools found mainly in the East, to the public High School as the main means of educating youth.

1892 and 1893 were landmark years for the American school curriculum. The National Education Association (NEA) put together a group known as the Committee of Ten, headed by Charles Eliot, the President of Harvard. The Committee's charge was to formulate a reasonable secondary school curriculum for American public schools. The curriculum shown in Figure 7.4 is the result of the Committee's work. Notice the emphasis on ancient languages as well as the emphasis on such "modern" subjects as physics, chemistry, and biology. This influential report signaled the beginning of the transition from perennialism to essentialism as the dominant form of the secondary curriculum.

Figure 7.4. High School Subject Time Allotments Recommended in the Committee of Ten Report (1893)

Subject	9th Year	10th Year	11th Year	12th Year
Latin	5/wk	5/wk	5/wk	5/wk
Greek	(Latin begun a year before Greek)	5/wk	4/wk	4/wk
English	3/wk Literature 2/wk Composition	3/wk Literature 2/wk Composition	3/wk Literature 1/wk Composition 1/wk Rhetoric	3/wk Literature 1/wk Composition 1/wk Grammar
Modern Languages (Elective German or French begun in 5th grade)	4/wk Language begun earlier	4/wk Language begun earlier 4/wk Add other language	4/wk Language begun earlier 4/wk Second language	4/wk Language begun earlier 4/wk Second language
Mathematics (Concrete Geometry Grades 5–8)	5/wk Algebra	2.5/wk Algebra or Bookkeeping and Commercial Arithmetic 2.5/wk Geometry	2.5/wk Algebra or Bookkeeping and Commercial Arithmetic 2.5/wk Geometry	Trigonometry and higher Algebra for candidates for scientific schools
Physics, Chemistry, & Astronomy Study of natural phenomena 5 p a wk through first eight years by experiments	5/wk for 12 wks Elective Astronomy	5/wk for 12 wks Elective Astronomy	5/wk Chemistry	5/wk Physics

Subject	9th Year	10th Year	11th Year	12th Year
Natural History (which year not specified)	One year: 5 botany or zoology		Half year: 5/wk anatomy, physiology, and hygiene	
History Greek/ Roman Gr. 8 American Gr 7 Biography & Mythology Gr 5–6	3/wk French History	3/wk English History	3/wk American History	3/wk A special period intensively, and civil government, Geography Time allotted in first eight years to equal that given to number work. The subject— the earth its environment and inhabitants, including the elements of astronomy, meteorology, zoölogy, botany, history, commerce, races, religions, and governments.
Physical Geography	Physiography, geology, or meteorology at some part of the high school course. Possibly more than one of these where election is allowed.)	Elective Meteorology, 1/2 this year or next	Elective geology or physiography, 1/2 yr	

Only twenty-five years later, another NEA-commissioned task force gave us the famous "Seven Cardinal Principles" report in which the rise of progressivism was clearly documented (see Figure 4.1).

Essentialism and perennialism are considered traditional philosophies of education and therefore of curriculum because they are rooted in authority. Essentialists and perennialists agree that students are not capable of deciding what they should study. A curriculum must be put together by experts and carried out by people of authority. Students need to learn the knowledge, skills, and values that conscientious adults have decided are needed for future success. Essentialists and perennialists view schooling as the training ground for adult life.

Discipline and order are hallmarks of these philosophies. Discipline takes the form of adult supervision as well as the self-control needed for serious study. Order takes the form of respect for adult authority, and it also takes the form of an orderly, preordained scope and sequence of course work. Academic standards in the form of achievement, tests, grades, and promotion based on merit are invariably found in essentialist and perennialist curriculums. The curriculum in either case is knowledge-centered.

While there is much overlap in these two world views, there is considerable difference as well. Essentialists embrace technology and applied learning far more than do perennialists. The essentialist will typically say that because society is changing, the course of study must adapt, for example, the inclusion of computer literacy in the curriculum or the placing of emphasis on skills that lead to jobs. The perennialist, on the other hand, will emphasize history, the humanities, and pure forms of mathematics and science as not only the source of eternal values but as ends in themselves.

Essentialists focus more on national interest, for example, the need for engineers, nurses, a strong military, while perennialists feel that these things will take care of themselves when a well-educated citizenry is produced. In one sense, the difference is that between a modern view of academic disciplines with all that entails versus a timeless view of virtue as the guide to the good life. To be sure, the essentialist will provide a rigorous course of study designed to produce productive citizens, while the perennialist will provide a rigorous course of study designed to produce enlightened citizens.

Of the two, essentialism is certainly a more dominant force in American education today. The essentialist call for basics, standards, testing, and a core knowledge curriculum is a call that has been well heeded in recent times. Perennialism, formerly the curriculum of elite education, is relatively minor player. Its greatest appeal has been to private preparatory (often religiously-based) schools.

These two conservative educational philosophies focus educational efforts on the future. Students are required to study a curriculum designed to prepare them for future study and work. Childhood and adolescence are a time in which students are asked to apply themselves less through expressed childhood interest than through effort that will lead to adult success, personally, socially, and professionally. This perspective stands in sharp contrast to the progressive perspective that places the focus on the present and on student interest.

Your Turn

Here is an excerpt from the first chapter of Charles Dickens' *Hard Times*. The speaker is Mr. Thomas Gradgrind, a merchant who has founded a model school. Gradgrind is speaking to Mr. McChoakumchild, a teacher in the model school. *Hard Times* was originally published in 1854.

Chapter One—The One Thing Needed

"Now, what I want is, Facts. Teach these boys and girls nothing but Facts. Facts alone are wanted in life. Plant nothing else, and root out everything else. You can only form the minds of reasoning animals upon Facts: nothing else will ever be of any service to them. This is the principle on which I bring up my own children, and this is the principle on which I bring up these children. Stick to Facts, sir!"

The scene was a plain, bare, monotonous vault of a schoolroom, and the speaker's square forefinger emphasized his observations by underscoring every sentence with a line on the schoolmaster's sleeve. The emphasis was helped by the speaker's square wall of a forehead, which had his eyebrows for its base, while his eyes found commodious cellarage in two dark caves, overshadowed by the wall. The emphasis was helped by the speaker's mouth, which was wide, thin, and hard set. The emphasis was helped by the speaker's hair, which bristled on the skirts of his bald head, a plantation of firs to keep the wind from its shining surface, all covered with knobs, like the crust of a plum pie, as if the head has scarcely warehouse-room for the hard facts stored inside. The speaker's obstinate carriage, square coat, square legs, square shoulders,…nay, his very neckcloth, trained to take him by the throat with an unaccommodating grasp, like a stubborn fact, as it was,…all helped the emphasis.

"In this life, we want nothing but Facts, sir; nothing but Facts."

The speaker, and the schoolmaster, and the third grown person present, all backed a little, and swept with their eyes the inclined plane of little vessels then and there arranged in order, ready to have imperial gallons of facts poured into them until they were full to the brim.

◆ What connections, if any, do you see to the current discussion?

Back to Bruner for a Minute

Jerome Bruner's ideas defy simple categorization, and unlike many knowledge-centered advocates, he has made a name for himself as an innovator, not a traditionalist. In fact, a number of knowledge-centered curriculum advocates think his focus on process is part of the problem in education (see Fig. 7.1).

Nevertheless, it does seem that some principles or ideas from Bruner's work inform the knowledge-centered curriculum in the most helpful of ways

The Structure of Knowledge Within a Discipline

Bruner takes issue with the performance orientation so popular today, saying that education should result in understanding and not merely in performance. His suggestion is that performance education sometimes is not really based on true understanding, something that Bruner suggests consists of grasping the structure of knowledge. He describes or defines the structure of knowledge within a discipline as having two major components.

The first component of *structure* is comprised of the key ideas or key concepts of a particular discipline. What are the key ideas of biology, literature, mathematics, or geography? This is one aspect of structure. Bruner encourages teachers to focus not on seemingly unrelated information, but on knowledge in the form of its essence, its wholeness, and its coherence. Think for a moment about a beautiful vase. Imagine it whole and imagine it broken into countless pieces. Its essence is found in its wholeness, its integrity, and not in a thousand shards of glass lying on the floor.

The other aspect of structure to which Bruner alludes is *method*. This raises the issue of what people who produce knowledge actually do. How they spend their time? What does a physicist, a painter, a writer do? On more than one occasion, Bruner has been asked the question, something along the lines of, 'are you trying to make little historians or little mathematicians out of these kids?' And Bruner's answer has been that this is exactly the point. Students do become authors, historians, and scientists as they actively engage in the processes of creating knowledge. Students learn the key ideas of history, of mathematics, of writing, etc., but they also practice the craft of scholarship, and that is what he means by understanding.

A related Brunerian idea, certainly not his alone, is that knowledge *discovered* is more useful to learners than knowledge merely received. Knowledge discovered builds on prior knowledge, whereas information from lectures or from a textbook doesn't necessarily take into account how much one already knows. For the discoverer what he or she already knows is crucial to what he or she can and will discover. Legend has it that Isaac Newton discovered gravity by being hit on the head by a falling apple, but many people have been hit on the head by falling apples without making a connection to universal laws of physics. In that sense, prior learning becomes the foundation for new learning. In other words, the more you know about something, the more you are able to learn on your own. The ability to learn on one's own is hardly a trivial commodity in life. This thought is highly touted by knowledge-centered advocates who underscore the importance of academic learning in the early years.

Another of Bruner's ideas is that the object of teaching and learning is not coverage, but depth. In that sense, Bruner is on the same page as the philosopher Alfred North Whitehead (1929) who recommended that teachers *teach less, not more.* Why? Because less is more. Don't try to cover too many subjects, is the way Whitehead put it. Go into great depth with the few powerful ideas that you do teach. If the ideas are not meaningful and powerful, you should not choose to teach them.

One of Bruner's better known contributions (and one that Hirsch takes issue with) is something known as the *spiral curriculum.* The idea of the spiral curriculum is that the key concepts and methods from each discipline are identified, and visited and revisited at increasing levels of sophistication throughout the school years. So, think of the curriculum as a spiral that keeps going back over the same concepts, but using different contexts, demanding increased understanding, employing different problems or content, and seriously taking into account prior knowledge and skill. At stake is something called schema theory, which suggests that knowledge builds on knowledge. Hirsch's main objection is Bruner's focus on spiraling concepts and skills, which he thinks is misguided. Hirsch favors knowledge, not elusive concepts and skills, as the building blocks of the curriculum.

Your Turn

Here is a quote from Bruner's book, *The Culture of Education* (1996, pp. 119, 120):

A long time ago, I proposed the concept of a "spiral curriculum," the idea that in teaching a subject you begin with an "intuitive" account that is well within the reach of a student, and then circle back later to a more formal or highly structured account, until, with however more recyclings are necessary, the learner has mastered the topic or subject in its full generative power. ... I had stated this more basic view in the form, almost, of a philosophical proverb, to the effect that "Any subject can be taught to any child at any age in some form that is honest." ... The research of the last three decades on the growth of reasoning in children has, in the main, confirmed the rightness of the spiral curriculum, although it has also provided us with some cautions.

- ◆ What is your opinion of the spiral curriculum, and what do you think the cautions are?

The Essentialist Paradigm

Look to the essence of a thing, whether it be point of doctrine, of practice, or of interpretation.

Marcus Aurelius

The essentialist approach to the curriculum is often labeled "traditional" or "basic." The essentialist movement began in earnest in the 1930s as a reaction to the perceived excesses of the progressive movement. It is also true that the progressive movement arose late in the 19th Century in large measure as a reaction to the "traditional" approach to schooling. For well over 100 years, essentialism and progressivism have played off one another, and each has become known not only for what it is but for what it is not. As John Dewey wrote (1938):

The rise of what is called the new education and progressive schools is of itself a product of discontent with traditional education. In effect it is a criticism of the latter.

Dewey described traditional education as a curriculum imposed from above and from outside. He argued that such a curriculum imposes adult standards and adult subject matter, by which he meant separate academic disciplines. He also criticized the methods used to teach the curriculum, noting that they were beyond the reach of children and more appropriately suited to adults undertaking advanced study. He went on to say that such a curriculum is as much folly as was the catastrophic cavalry charge of the British Light Brigade chronicled in poetry by Alfred Lord Tennyson. Since the Light Brigade were slaughtered by the enemy, these are strong words indeed.

By the 1930s advocates of the traditional approaches so caricatured and ridiculed by Dewey had seen enough of the progressive influence in America's schools. Under the leadership of William Chandler Bagley, a professor of education at Columbia University Teachers College, the traditionalists formed their own organization, the Council on Basic Education. The counter-movement formed by the Council came to be known as essentialism. It is time, essentialists argued, to go back to the basics.

The Essentialist Curriculum

The essentialist curriculum is one of "essential" skills and knowledge. It is a future-oriented curriculum in that it asks, "what knowledge and skills will students need to prepare them for future life?" But it is also a past-oriented curriculum in that it advocates a return to the "higher standards" of the past. By way of contrast, the progressive paradigm is present-oriented, stating boldly that school is not preparation for life, but life itself, as Dewey remarked on more than one occasion. In spite of all this, both essentialists and progressives would argue that theirs is the best preparation for life in an unknown future.

In its most pure form, an essentialist curriculum is organized into separate subjects that correspond to the time-honored scholarly academic disciplines. The idea is that basic literacy is the best preparation for students facing an unknown future. The idea is to have them receive a broad, liberal education that includes literature, grammar, science, mathematics, history and geography, in other words, an academic education. Particularly at secondary levels, where separate subjects are taught by specialists, there is typically little connection made between or among subjects. Even at primary levels, separate subjects are taught although typically by one teacher.

At elementary levels, an essentialist curriculum often makes certain concessions to progressivism, combining several subjects into one, for example, language arts, which includes grammar, spelling, penmanship, literature, reading (as in phonics), writing, speaking, and listening. However, little effort is made to connect language arts with other subjects as progressives advocate. A problematic issue is that elementary teachers are not specialists but generalists who are called upon to teach a wide range of subject matter. A point of contention is at what age level it becomes appropriate for children to attend separate classes taught by specialists.

The essentialist curriculum is generally textbook-based. Even at first grade level, the essentialist will cite the need for a basal reader that promotes skill development in phonics, while the progressive will typically argue for a "real books" whole language approach. Essentialist teachers use textbook guides or teachers' editions that are specially prepared to regulate the flow of instruction and study. Because textbooks, at least at the elementary level are usually adopted as a series, an orderly scope (breadth of coverage) and sequence (chronology of coverage) is established, ensuring that important topics are introduced at appropriate times. In this sense, the curriculum is conceived of as an object, something apart from students and teachers interests. Because it arrives at school as a finished product, the textbook does not cater to local needs or interests.

An essentialist curriculum need not be textbook-dominated, although it typically is. The many problems associated with textbooks have been chronicled time and again. Critics cite shortcomings ranging from the many errors often found in them to the bland and uninteresting way in which knowledge and skills are presented. Textbooks in schools are so ubiquitous that such critics as historian Diane Ravitch have pointed out that in the United States we do have a national curriculum. Three states (California, Texas, and Florida) account for something on the order of 30% of textbook sales, and those states set the tone for the many other states where textbook adoptions are common. Also, four publishers (McGraw-Hill, Harcourt, Houghton Mifflin, and Pearson) control perhaps seventy percent of the market (Center for Educational Reform 2001). So, for better or worse, essentialism as has achieved curricular dominance in American public education, at least in so far as essentialism is personified by the textbook.

Teacher Role

The teacher's role in an essentialist curriculum is one of director of learning. The center of gravity lies with the teacher, since the assumption is that he or she is a mature adult in possession of far greater mastery of the subject matter and the ways of delivering it than are the students. The teacher represents adult authority and is thought to be in a better position than are children to make judgments about what knowledge and skills are crucial to a purposeful fife. Figure 7.5 lists features of essentialist curriculum.

Figure 7.5. Features of an Essentialist Curriculum

Emphasis	◆ Basic skills and knowledge focus ◆ Textbook orientation ◆ Prescribed scope and sequence ◆ Focus on content ◆ Separate subjects emphasis
Teaching	◆ Direct instruction ◆ Teacher-centered ◆ Traditional teaching ◆ Teacher as authority ◆ Teacher as subject matter expert
Learning	◆ Acquisition of knowledge and skills ◆ Teacher initiated and directed ◆ Independent work ◆ Competitive
Environment	◆ Clear academic focus ◆ Traditional discipline ◆ School as workplace
Assessment	◆ Age-graded classes ◆ Specialized ◆ Departmentalized ◆ Standard tests ◆ Letter grades

Direct instruction by the teacher is typical, although accommodation is made for projects, independent study, group work, and other pedagogical devices that make learning more appealing to the young. The teacher is responsible for assessing learning, and letter grades as well as academic promotion are in his or her hands. In all, the teacher directs, not facilitates, learning.

Student Role

Students are expected to acquire academic skills and knowledge in an essentialist curriculum. Such values as self-discipline, effort, and participation in the course of study are fully expected. Students typically have little say either in charting the course of the curriculum. These are matters better left to adult authority. So, such matters as student planning, choice of what and how to study, and self assessment are largely absent. The student's job is to learn the material and complete the assignments. To be fair, choices often do exist within a well-prescribed framework. But there is little of the free-form style of the progressive classroom. The typical image is of the teacher in front of the whole class, teaching a lesson.

Critics of essentialism claim that the student's role is that of passive learner. It is true that a typical progressive classroom has more student activity than does a typical essentialist classroom. But to be fair to essentialism, one does find a certain amount of group activity, project work, construction, and student movement about the classroom. Essentialists will argue that their emphasis is upon an active mind, not merely on moving around. They claim that a rigorous academic curriculum represents the best form of activity because it challenges the mind. Whether this argument holds up is a matter of opinion.

Organization of the Curriculum

The essentialist classroom and school generally lends itself to an age-graded organization in which promotion is based on achievement. This has been the tradition since the mid Century when Horace Mann (Cremin 1957) advised that schools be organized this way in the wake of his visit to Germany where he first encountered this arrangement. Essentialists tend to view such innovations as continuous progress, nongraded school organization, etc., as little more than faddish distractions from the real issue of raising academic achievement. Curiously, where continuous progress is taken seriously, it often is found in a curriculum of worksheets and criterion tests, pure essentialism. Progressives point to such circumstances as perversions of the idea of continuous progress.

The curriculum is also organized by subject matter, in the form of a daily schedule of classes taught by one or two teachers at elementary levels and by subject matter specialists at secondary levels. Because the clear emphasis is on academic achievement, ability grouping is a common phenomenon, ranging from reading groups at primary levels to tracking at secondary levels. At the elementary level, ability grouping is done while keeping homeroom arrangements intact. Reading groups, for example, occupy different corners of the room. At intermediate levels, students may be shuffled into perhaps high, middle, and low mathematics groups taught by the teachers at a given grade level. These are the beginnings of ability grouping. However, at the secondary level, we encounter one of the basic tenets of essentialism, and that is the sorting and tracking of students by academic ability. In a large comprehensive high school, this means a college-bound preparatory track, a middle of the road track, and a vocational track.

Assessment

Assessment tends to take the form of letter grades, marked papers, standard tests, report cards, and teacher judgment of pupil progress. Assessment, like planning, is largely in the hands of the teacher and other experts. Although formative assessment can and often does play a role in evaluation and diagnosis, emphasis is placed on summative assessments ranging from end-of-term examinations to scores on standardized tests. Social promotion, an idea advanced by progressives, is frowned upon by essentialist purists. The present-day standards movement and the push to test all children is evidence of the influence of essentialist educational thought and practice.

Thinking About Essentialism

One way to think about an essentialist curriculum is to view it as a "back to basics" model. This oversimplifies the situation somewhat, but not entirely. The idea of back to basics is predicated on the assumption that the curriculum once was founded in basics but somehow lost its way. This is indeed central to the essentialist argument, and the culprit, the philosophy that came to school and changed things for the worse, is progressivism. In fact the essentialist movement, which one might erroneously assume is older than progressivism, is younger. It came into being in the 1930s as a reaction to the perceived excesses of progressivism and progressivism's foundational element, pragmatism.

Columbia University professor William Chandler Bagley, in an address to the National Education Association's annual meeting in 1938, clarified the essentialist position with his emphasis on the following points:

- ◆ American students fail to meet the standards of achievement attained by students in other countries.

- ◆ An increasing number of high school students are basically illiterate.

- ◆ Notable deficiencies exist in mathematics and grammar throughout the grades.

♦ More money is being spent on education than ever before, but such problems as the crime rate continue to increase.

These same themes have been replayed like a broken record at education conferences and in state legislatures in every year since then. Bagley and other essentialists then and now point to the folly of "life adjustment" courses, inordinate emphases on the extra curriculum, educational fads such as learning styles and self-esteem, and other distractions from the real purpose of school, which is to emphasize basic knowledge, attitudes, and skills.

Essentialism refers, as you might imagine, to that which is essential. Essential things are things we cannot do without. So, just as certain things are basic to our very existence, air, water, food, shelter, etc., so are certain school subjects basic to a student's existence. Those basics typically include reading, writing, mathematics, science, history, civics, and geography, or what might be called literacy and numeracy. The lists of what should be left in and what left out vary slightly, depending on who is putting the list together, but the subjects named above are certainly widely agreed on as essential. The arts are included on some lists, and are left out of others.

The essentialist point of view refers to more than the subjects themselves. It also includes a clear view of social/moral propriety and issues of character development. Essentialists such as E. D. Hirsch, Jr., chief architect of the Core Knowledge Curriculum, and William Bennett, editor of the bestseller, *The Book of Virtues*, both address through story and other forms, matters of value-positive character development. Among the character qualities stressed by essentialists are discipline and effort, respect for others and for property, goal setting, postponement of immediate gratification, democracy and individual rights and responsibilities, among other related values. While Hirsch is clearly in the essentialist camp, Bennett is perhaps as much perennialist as essentialist.

Is an Essentialist Curriculum a Match for Your School?

If you found yourself in general agreement with the profile just sketched, then it probably is something you will seriously wish to consider. If you do see yourself as an essentialist, you will find that you have some well-known educational thinkers on your side. Among those who have argued strongly for an essentialist curriculum are Arthur Bestor, author of the critically acclaimed book, *Educational Wastelands* (1953), William C. Bagley, the founder of the essentialist movement, E. D. Hirsch, Jr. whose Core Knowledge Curriculum is in use in a number of settings, and Admiral Hyman Rickover, whose criticisms of progressive education were particularly pointed.

E. D. Hirsch Jr's. Core Knowledge Curriculum

Essentialism

The Core Knowledge Sequence for grades K–8 is a guide to the curriculum's significant content. Unlike most curriculum guides, which list goals, skills, and general learning outcomes, the Core Knowledge sequence lists specific content to be learned by grade level. The curriculum identifies four aspects or attributes of a common core of knowledge, that it is:

- ◆ shared,
- ◆ solid,
- ◆ sequenced, and
- ◆ specific.

Shared knowledge is at the foundation of what Hirsch has called "cultural literacy." It is not enough for a few to know mathematics, history, literature, etc. The argument is that everyone in the culture must hold important knowledge in common to make the claim that indeed we have a common culture. Without such common knowledge of everything from nursery rhymes to geometry, there can be no real communication

By "solid knowledge" the Core Knowledge Sequence means lasting, important knowledge, including traditions, discoveries, inventions, stories, myths, and a range of other knowledge from science, mathematics, history, literature, the arts, and geography. The solid knowledge argument is particularly one against the progressive insistence on the teaching and learning of free-standing skills and content-free critical thinking abilities

Sequenced knowledge, as the term implies, means building new knowledge on existing knowledge. In one sense, this is similar to the idea of the spiral curriculum where ideas are visited and revisited at increasing levels of sophistication and complexity. However, Core Knowledge proponents shun such comparisons, insisting instead on a focus on specific knowledge sequenced in some coherent fashion, for example, studying ancient Greece prior to a study of Rome, or learning addition prior to learning multiplication.

Specific knowledge means identifying important terms, names, dates, events, and discoveries and ensuring that those historic facts are studied. Of course, the curriculum is based on specific knowledge that is deemed crucial to a child's understanding of the world and particularly of his or her own culture with its traditions, stories, and history. This, too, represents a major departure from progressive curriculum theory which argues that any specific knowledge is arbitrary and that teachers and students ought to be able to select the kind of content they wish to study.

An Elitist Curriculum?

The Core Knowledge shares a number of things in common with Mortimer Adler's Paideia, and one of them is the accusation that they are both elitist, Eurocentric curriculums. Hirsch, like Adler, denies this. He argues that his curriculum is actually more democratic, less elitist, than curriculums that demand less of students and teachers. Hirsch is convinced that the knowledge currently possessed only by the elite should be made available to all children through the one institution available to all, the public school. Hirsch, like Adler, claims that progressive curriculums are in fact elitist in that they do not emphasize the high academic standards for all that are necessary to future success, either in advanced study or in the world of work. The Eurocentric charge, certainly related to the elitist charge, is more problematic in one sense. A review of the content does lead one to conclude that most of it comes from the Western World, its history, cultures, stories, etc.

However, to be fair to the curriculum, Core Knowledge does in fact cover the Eastern World, other cultures, and contributions of minorities to civilization. See Figure 7.6 for an example of a Curriculum Unit based on Core Knowledge Content.

Figure 7.6. Example of Essentialist Curriculum:
Core Knowledge

American Civilization Grade 2*	
General Topics and Guidelines ♦ Lives and accomplishments of important Americans ♦ Timelines for grasping chronology	
Specific Content	
American government based on a constitution	
(Only the concept needs to be introduced at this time; more detailed study of the Constitution begins in grade 4)	♦ James Madison, "Father of the Constitution"
War of 1812	♦ President Madison, ♦ Dolley Madison; ♦ Old Ironsides; ♦ British burn the White House and Capitol; ♦ Fort McHenry, ♦ Francis Scott Key, "The Star-Spangled Banner"
Westward Expansion	♦ Pioneers; ♦ New means and routes of travel: ♦ Erie Canal; railroads; ♦ Robert Fulton, invention of the steamboat;
War with Mexico	♦ The Alamo ("Remember the Alamo") Texas; ♦ Davy Crockett; ♦ Jim Bowie

Native Americans	◆ Forced removal to reservations; ◆ Sioux; ◆ Sitting Bull; ◆ Crazy Horse; ◆ Little Bighorn, Custer's Last Stand; ◆ Apache; ◆ Geronimo
The "Wild West"	◆ Buffalo Bill, Annie Oakley (Note: In grade 5, students take up the question of reality versus legend in the "Wild West")
Civil War	◆ Controversy over slavery; ◆ Harriet Tubman, the "Underground Railroad"; ◆ Lincoln: story of "Honest Abe"
20th Century	◆ Civil Rights Marches; ◆ Rosa Parks, Martin Luther King, Jr.; ◆ Boycott; ◆ Man on the moon
Symbols and Figures	◆ Stars and Stripes; ◆ Uncle Sam; ◆ Statue of Liberty, poem inscribed on it ("Give me your tired, your poor...")

Student Role

The role of the student in the Core Knowledge Curriculum is that of knowledge acquisition. The content of the curriculum is clearly spelled out, and students are clearly expected to acquire it. The pedagogical perspective of the Core Knowledge Curriculum is that general knowledge is the best entrée to deep knowledge. That is, the role of the young learner (K–8) is to become acquainted with the general principles and numerous examples of subject matter from the traditional academic disciplines. Hirsch makes the point that the general ability of a student to learn is highly correlated with his or her general knowledge. Thus a broad range of subjects, not just the three R's, but science, history, geography, civics, ethics, the arts, and literature are crucial to a student's ability to become an independent-thinking, well-informed, participating citizen who shares a body of knowledge (cultural literacy) with his or her fellow citizens.

Teacher Role

The teacher in a Core Knowledge classroom is required to follow the syllabus, to teach the core knowledge as it is defined. It is not expected of the teacher that he or she becomes a walking data bank, but that he or she is genuinely interested in the subject matter of the curriculum. This interest is manifested in teacher learning and modeling and in a clear expectation that students come to school wanting to learn. The curriculum stresses content knowledge, to be sure, but it is a misconception to think that the teacher's role is merely to teach isolated facts from a prepared list. Direct instruction is expected, but not that alone. Ideally, the teacher assumes an interactive role in guiding and presenting experiences and instruction. But there is no escaping the fact that the teacher must be a scholar in the sense of taking the subject matter seriously. The students need to see in their teacher a person who values academic knowledge.

Assessment

Student work and progress are assessed in fairly traditional terms. Tests, letter grades, and promotion based on achievement are basic elements of the program. However, the Core Knowledge Curriculum does make room for "authentic assessment" in the form of projects, activities, performances, and anecdotal reporting.

Your Turn

The essentialist model focuses heavily on those aspects of curricula that are easy to measure: knowledge and skills. Some would argue that this simple focus is what allowed its reform efforts to be so successful.

♦ What are your thoughts on the current controversy of standardized tests of essential knowledge? Draw on what you have already thought about all three 'centers' of curriculum: learner, society, and knowledge.

The Perennialist Paradigm

> The three greatest metaphysicians who ever lived are Plato, Aristotle, and St. Thomas Aquinas.
>
> *Etienne Gilson*

If education were a three-ring circus, perennialism would not be found in the center ring. Neither would it be relegated to the status of sideshow simply because it is a serious educational philosophy that ought not to be subjected to caricature. Its historical prominence is considerable, although its present-day status makes it nearly unknown to some educators who are far more familiar with the more dominant essentialist view of the curriculum. Therefore, this section dedicates enough space to acquaint you with the basic tenets of perennialism without explicating it to the extent that I do essentialism.

Perennialists believe that the purpose of education is the cultivation of the mind though the study of permanent (perennial) truths to be found in the classical studies. Great ideas, lasting truths, and rational thinking are cornerstones of a perennialist curriculum. Perennialism dominated American education from Colonial times through the 19th Century, but it has been greatly marginalized in our times, eclipsed by both the essentialist and progressive movements. Perennialist educational philosophy reaches back to Ancient Greece and the work of Plato and Aristotle, and to Thomas Aquinas in the Middle Ages. It is in fact, a blend of Greek and Christian influence that held sway in education for centuries but that has been pushed aside in a more secular age.

The best known example of perennialist education today is found in higher education, at St. Johns College (Annapolis, MD and Santa Fe, NM), where students study the works of the great thinkers of Western Civilization. The best known example at the school level (K–12) is Mortimer Adler's *Paideia* curriculum, which is explicated in detail following this brief overview. It would indeed be difficult to find many, if any, American public schools today practicing a perennialist educational philosophy. Where perennialism does prosper at the school level, it is in a few private, primarily Christian, schools.

A perennialist curriculum consists mainly of studies in grammar, logic, rhetoric, writing, history, mathematics, foreign language, and the Great Books, as they are called. The purpose of the curriculum is to educate students who know such lasting truths as goodness, happiness, courage, duty, honor, liberty, responsibility, citizenship, and others. This is done through reading and discussion, especially Socratic dialogue, writing, and learning the foundations of rational argument. In this sense, a true perennialist curriculum is a combination of didactic teaching and ongoing conversation between teachers and students.

Perennialists are convinced that modern education has been corrupted by losing sight of first principles, that is, perennial ideas. For perennialists, essentialism is too pragmatic and eclectic to be of much help beyond training students rather than educating them. Progressives, on the other hand, are too worried about adult authority, which perennialists see as a solution rather than a problem. The progressive inclination to invest in the child such character traits as goodness and wisdom strikes perennialists as not merely naive but dangerous. A perennialist curriculum is not a curriculum of choice, indirection, activity for its own sake, or even simply one of basic skills. Rather, it is a curriculum designed to acquaint students with the thinking of the best minds of the ages.

Perhaps the most familiar argument today against perennialism is that it is elitist, undemocratic, and suited only to a select few. The perennialist counter-argument is, to quote Robert Maynard Hutchins, "the best education for the best is the best education for all." In fact, most perennialists support a one-track educational system with the same course of study for every student. Their claim is that, regardless of whether a student goes on to higher education, the world of work, the military, or anything else, that student deserves an education that equips him or her to continue on as a lifelong learner. The perennialist sees this philosophy of schooling as society's best hope of preserving and improving its democratic institutions.

Not everyone, of course, would agree. Theodore Brameld (1955) called perennialism a threat to democracy. He wrote, "Perennialism is not only unsound but also dangerous, threatening our contention that the revitalization of democracy is the most pressing obligation facing contemporary mankind" (p. 289). Brameld contended that the result of a widespread use of perennialist educational ideas would be the rise of an aristocracy of "high-minded directors of the masses" and/or a corruption and abuse of authority by the few. Most essentialists and progressives tend to view perennialism as a relic of the educational past, hardly worth serious attention.

Mortimer Adler's Paideia Curriculum

Perennialism

> There are no unteachable children. There are only schools and teachers and parents who fail to teach them.
>
> *Mortimer Adler*

Mortimer Adler was a philosopher and educator who held to a perennialist view of schooling as being the fairest, most democratic way of educating the young in our society. The oft-quoted statement of Adler's colleague, Robert Maynard Hutchins, "the best education for the best is the best education for all," means a rigorous academic curriculum for every child composed of challenging subject matter. For Adler, the source of the curriculum is found in the great ideas that have shaped the best that civilization has to offer. Such ideas as democracy, happiness, good and evil, honor, wisdom, time and space, and citizen, are at the core of the curriculum. These ideas are explicated in the Great Books of the Western World series that Adler himself edited. In that program, which was developed as a kind of lifelong reading plan, the reader is exposed to the thoughts of Homer, Aristotle, Plato, Shakespeare, Milton, Newton, Kant, and others.

In his book, The Paideia Proposal (1982), Adler set forth his ideas for a school curriculum based on a classical, humanist education. The word *paideia* is of Greek origin, referring to the upbringing of a child. It is related to the terms pedagogy and pediatrics. As he notes in the acknowledgement to the book, "in an extended sense, [*paideia* is] the equivalent of the Latin *humanitas*... signifying the general learning that should be in the possession of all human beings. In this sense, the *paideia* curriculum is designed to offer a general, liberal education to school students."

Roberts and Billings (1999), who direct the National Paideia Center, write that the three goals of schooling should be to prepare students to earn a livelihood, become good citizens, and make a good life. They note that the purpose of school is to help make this possible by offering students the opportunity to acquire organized knowledge, form habits of skill, and experience growth of the mind. See Figure 7.7 for a fill listing of the Paideia Principles.

Figure 7.7. The Paideia Principles

The Paideia Principles

- All children can learn.
- All children deserve the same quality schooling, not just the same quantity.
- The quality of schooling to which all children are entitled is what the wisest parents would wish for their own children, the best education for the best being the best education of all.
- Schooling is the best preparation for becoming generally educated in the course of a whole lifetime, and schools should be judged on how well they provide such preparation.
- The three callings for which schooling should prepare all Americans are:
  - to earn a decent livelihood;
  - to be a good citizen of the nation and the world; and
  - to make a good life for one's self.
- The primary cause of genuine learning is the activity of the learner's own mind, sometimes with the help of a teacher functioning as a secondary and cooperative cause.
- The three types of teaching that should occur in our schools are didactic teaching of subject matter; coaching that produces the skills of learning; and Socratic questioning in seminar discussion.
- The results of these three types of teaching should be the acquisition of organized knowledge; the formation of habits of skill in the use of language and mathematics, and the growth of the mind's understanding of basic ideas and issues.
- Each student's achievement of these results would be evaluated in terms of that student's competencies and not solely related to the achievements of other students.
- The principal of the school should never be a mere administrator, but always a leading teacher who should be cooperatively engaged with the school's teaching staff in planning, reforming, and reorganizing the school as an educational community.
- The principal and faculty of a school should themselves be actively engaged in learning.

◆ The desire to continue their own learning should be the prime motivation of those who dedicate their lives to the profession of teaching.

Unequivocally, this is a curriculum of considerable academic challenge with no elective courses, no vocational track, no sorting of students by ability. Adler's belief was that nearly all students, with very few exceptions, are capable of learning. He writes, "True, children are educable in varying degrees, but the variation in degree must be of the same kind and quality of education" (1982, p. 7). Adler had no objection to vocational training and specialization, but he was convinced that such matters ought not to be part of the K–12 experience. All that could and should come later.

The Paideia curriculum is comprised of integrated units of study in which teachers and students explore ideas through direct instruction, expert coaching, and seminars. The idea behind the use of the three modes is to ensure curricular/instructional balance through the exploration of a core curriculum based on classic works of history, literature, politics, etc., great ideas in science and mathematics, and the engagement of subject matter through lecture, reading, inquiry, debate, performance, artistic expression, physical activity and health, and problem solving. See Figure 7.8 for a listing of what Adler called the "three columns of learning," that is, instruction, coaching, and seminars.

Figure 7.8. The "Three Columns" of Balanced Paideia Teaching Method

	Didactic Instruction	Coaching	Seminar
Emphasis	Acquisition of factual knowledge	Development of intellectual skills	Increased Understanding of Ideas and Values
Teaching	Lecture, demonstration, videos, and reading	Guidance through modeling and questioning	Collaborative, intellectual dialogue facilitated by open-ended questions about a text
Time Balance	10%–15%	60%–70%	15%–20%
Assessment	Traditional short answer and multiple choice tests	Performance tasks, project work often with the use of check-lists and rubrics	Pre- and post-seminar tools and processes including self identified goals, discussion, and writing.

The Paideia Classroom

A Paideia classroom features these three interrelated teaching/learning approaches, or what Adler termed, "columns": Instruction, Coaching, and Seminars.

♦ *Didactic Instruction*

The first column, *Instruction*, is implemented in the form of teacher-directed activities. This includes didactic teaching or direct instruction, including lecture, presentation, and demonstration. In addition to the teacher's shared knowledge, textbooks in language, literature, the arts, sciences, mathematics, history, geography, and social studies are the centerpiece of this aspect of curriculum. This might be thought of from a curricular point of view as knowledge received or organized knowledge acquired through traditional methods.

◆ *Coaching*

The second technique, *Coaching*, involves skill development through supervised practice and activities. In a basic sense, coaching involves the practical application of knowledge. Students become involved in inquiry, problem solving, speaking, listening, and critiquing, under the teacher's expert guidance. The analogy with athletics is obvious in the use of the term "coaching." The coach observes, demonstrates, corrects, advises, supports, and otherwise nurtures, but it is the players (students) who must do the performing. Cooperative learning and peer coaching are often integrated into this approach as well. Coaching is a form of "learning by doing," an innovative aspect of the curriculum that Paideia's critics seem often to overlook (see Figure 7.8).

◆ Seminars

The third of Paideia's techniques represents formal discussion groups based on reading and related research. The teacher leads the seminar but must do so by playing the role of questioner, thought provoker, and drawer-out. This is not lecture time. The Socratic method of questioning is central to a seminar's success. Students must participate actively, using arguments drawn from knowledge they have acquired and critically examined. Seminar topics reflect the range of the curriculum, from the arts and sciences to the humanities.

Teacher Role

The teacher's role in the Paideia curriculum is that of *scholar/director* of learning. The role, particularly as it is conceived with respect to coaching students, has been characterized as being "like that of the master craftsman at work surrounded by apprentices. In this role, the teacher works with students, helping them perfect their skills so that the end product of their common labor is of the highest quality." (Roberts and Billings, 1999)

This is all much harder than it may seem. The teacher must strike the strategic balance between knowing a great deal and allowing young people to develop their own knowledge. It is all too tempting for the well-schooled teacher to think that telling is teaching; and all too tempting to the poorly-schooled teacher to allow students to learn on their own. In fact, this may well account for a key reason that the Paideia curriculum is not more widespread. The teacher is expected to know a great deal about subject matter and he or she is expected to share that knowledge through traditional means, but beyond that, through the kinds of coaching that only a master can provide, and through the expert "guide on the side" facilitation of discussion so necessary to the success of the seminars.

Student Role

The student, like the teacher, is expected to engage in serious scholarship. High academic standards are clearly present. The student is expected to acquire a general, liberal education. This is the goal of the program. Students do not specialize, even at the secondary level; rather, they are expected to acquire a liberal education that includes no vocational courses and basically no electives (a choice of foreign language is sometimes allowed). Students are expected to do more than acquire knowledge, however. They are expected to engage in performance and a range of forms of active learning. And the seminar approach puts them into active discussion, debate, and the give and take that emerges when people are allowed to express their ideas openly and civilly.

Schoolwide Leadership

The Paideia curriculum is, as its architects point out, a serious academic course of study, one that is liberal, not vocational; general, not specialized, and humanistic, not technical. This approach calls for "a principal who is truly the principal teacher in that school, who works with the teaching staff and is their educational leader, not just the school's chief administrative officer" (Adler 1984, p. 7).

These are exacting demands. Paideia calls upon the principal to champion the program through modeling, teaching, and clearly communicating a vision of academic excellence. As a model, the principal must him/herself be a scholar, a person who is well read, and passionate about ideas. Faculty meetings must be about the nature of knowledge, ways to nurture academic growth, and about how to ensure that the program goes forward.

The principal must model good teaching. He/she must spend time in classrooms, taking the role of teacher from time to time. Ideally, the principal should be teaching at least one class on a regular basis as a means of modeling and keeping in touch with faculty and students. The principal, like every teacher on the staff, should take part in the three column obligation of instruction, coaching, and seminars.

In many respects, the principal's role is closer to that of academic dean than chief administrative officer. Of course, a school needs administrative leadership, but Paideia asks more of the leader than merely that. Paideia demands scholarship

The National Paideia Center

The National Paideia Center, located at the University of North Carolina at Greensboro, acts as a clearing house and resource center for the Paideia approach to education. Any school seriously interested in exploring the possibilities of using this curriculum would do well to consult the Center for ideas on support, materials, teacher training, and assessment.

Your Turn

The Paideia model recommends balancing the three types of learning experience this way: no more than 20 percent didactic instruction, at least 20 percent seminars, and approximately 60 percent coaching of projects that use the didactic instruction.

- ◆ What do you think of this balance?
- ◆ What theory and research from educational psychology would support or refute this approach?

The International Baccalaureate Diploma Programme

A Worldwide Curriculum

Why do people go to college? In an idealistic world, they might go to develop a capacity for critical thinking, enhance an already grounded knowledge of the sciences and world culture, learn further how to deal with other people's diversity of opinion and, background, and in general become better citizens. They might go for fun, for friendship, or for a network of contacts. They might go for spiritual enrichment or for pragmatic honing of skills. In the real world, though, mostly they go to college to make money.

William A. Henry, III

Overview and Philosophy

The International Baccalaureate Organization (IBO) describes its curriculum as "a rigorous pre-university course of studies that leads to examinations, for highly motivated secondary students" (www.ibo.org). The IBO curriculum certainly qualifies as a knowledge-centered, academically-oriented curriculum. Its purpose is to prepare students for the academic challenges of university life. Perhaps we can agree that it is a knowledge-centered curriculum that attempts to take into account the global societal demands made on students in an ever changing world. Certainly, its stated goal of developing international understanding among students of many cultures speaks to a certain society-centered emphasis, but it is clearly an academic, university preparatory curriculum.

The IBO, is a nonprofit educational foundation based in Geneva, Switzerland, established to offer students around the world a *Diploma Programme* in the final two years of high school, ages 16 to 19, a *Middle Years Programme* for students ages 11 to 16, and the *Primary Years Programme* for students ages 3 to 12. The IBO has authorized 1300 schools in 110 countries to teach these programs.

From its inception in 1968 (the first full year of operation was 1970), the International Baccalaureate *Diploma Programme* was designed to cater to the educational needs of students attending international schools. The idea was to develop a curriculum, which might represent a compromise between the specialized regimen of national curricula, and the more broad concerns that outsiders possessed. Having an established high school curriculum available worldwide made sense in an era of growing multinational corporations and mobile families.

Three principles governed the development of the Programme:

1. the need for broad general education utilizing basic knowledge and critical thinking skills necessary for further learning;
2. the importance of developing international understanding;
3. the need for flexibility of choice among the subjects to be studied.

Alec Peterson, one of the founders and author of *Schools Across Frontiers* (2003), wanted to be sure to emphasize process rather than content. Like Whitehead, he believed that the general aim of education was not the acquisition of knowledge, but the development of general powers of mind. What the IBO program now details as its distinctive overall aims are the following:

- ◆ to provide an internationally accepted qualification for entry into higher education anywhere in the world;
- ◆ to promote international understanding;
- ◆ to educate the whole person, emphasizing intellectual, personal, emotional, and social growth;
- ◆ To develop inquiry and thinking skills and the capacity to reflect upon and to evaluate actions critically.

The Diploma Programme Curriculum Model

The curriculum today is represented as a hexagon model, with six academic areas surrounding a core. Students study six subjects selected from six subject groups, concurrently over two years, as well as the core elements of the program (theory of knowledge; the extended essay; and creativity, action, service). This is illustrated in the IBO Programme Model (see Fig. 6.2).

Figure 7.9. International Baccalaureate Programme Model

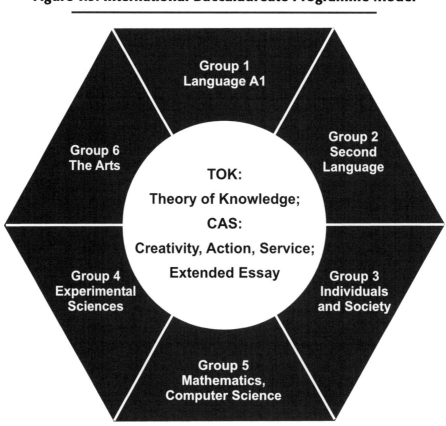

Group 1
Language A1

Group 2
Second
Language

Group 6
The Arts

TOK:
Theory of Knowledge;
CAS:
Creativity, Action, Service;
Extended Essay

Group 4
Experimental
Sciences

Group 3
Individuals
and Society

Group 5
Mathematics,
Computer Science

Subject Choices

The six subject groups represent the major domains of learning across all subject disciplines of a curriculum. At least three, and not more than four of the six subjects selected are taken at higher level (HL), the others at standard level (SL). HL courses represent 240 teaching hours, and require a greater depth of study across a broader range of content in the subject. SL courses require 150 hours and provide breadth of study across the whole Diploma Programme. Within this model, students are able to explore some subjects in depth and some more broadly over the two-year period. Most subjects are available at both HL and SL and can be taught and examined in English, French, or Spanish.

♦ Group 1. Language A1—First language, including the study of selections of world literature. Forty-five languages are regularly available; others are available on request.

- Group 2. Language A2, B, *ab initio*—second modern language courses for various levels of proficiency; classical languages.

- Group 3. Individuals and societies—history, geography, economics, philosophy, psychology, social and cultural anthropology, business and management, information technology in a global society (SL only), Islamic history.

- Group 4. Experimental Sciences—biology, chemistry, physics, environmental systems (SL only), design technology.

- Group 5. Mathematics and computer science—Mathematics (HL only), mathematical methods (SL only), mathematical studies (SL only), further mathematics (SL only), computer science (elective).

- Group 6. The arts—visual arts, music, and theater arts.

In Figure 7.10 (page 142) is an example of an English Syllabus for Group 1 Language A1. This would be designed for a two-year sequence including summer reading before grades 11 and 12.

Figure 7.10. Example of IBO Curriculum Unit Theme (Social Responsibility)

Syllabus for A1 English (2003–2005) *IBO Theme: Social Moral Responsibility*				
	Part 1 Works: World Literature	*Part 2 Works: Detailed Study*	*Part 3 Works: Genre Studies (poetry)*	*Part 4 Works: (School's Choice)*
Summer before 11	*Death of a Salesman*			
Grade 11		*Oedipus Divine Comedy Brothers Karamazov*	*Metamorphosis,* Ovid	*The Sun Also Rises*
Summer before 12				*The Things They Carried*
Grade 12		Annie Dillard, Selected Essays *Hamlet* Pound, *Selected Cantos The Dubliners,* Joyce	Selected Poems Frost Eliot Keats	The Iliad

The Core of the IBO Programme

As illustrated in Figure 7.9 (page 140), the core of the model consists of the Theory of Knowledge (TOK) course, the extended essay, and creativity, action, service (CAS).

The interdisciplinary TOK course is designed to provide coherence by exploring the nature of knowledge across all disciplines, encouraging an appreciation of other cultural perspectives. The extended essay, with a prescribed limit of 4000 words, offers the opportunity to investigate a topic of individual interest, and acquaints students with the independent research and writing skills expected at tertiary level. Participation in the school's CAS program encourages students to be involved in artistic pursuits, sports and community service work, thus fostering their awareness and appreciation of life outside the academic arena.

Theory of Knowledge

The Theory of Knowledge (TOK) offers students and their teachers the opportunity to reflect critically on diverse ways of knowing and on areas of knowledge. To this end, TOK is composed almost entirely of questions. The most central of these questions is "How do we know?" All subjects around the hexagon aim to encourage in all students an appreciation and understanding of cultures and attitudes other than their own, but in this particular respect, TOK has a special role to play. It is a stated aim of TOK that students should become aware of the *interpretative nature* of knowledge, including personal and ideological biases, regardless of whether, ultimately, these biases are retained, revised or rejected. TOK also has an important role to play in providing coherence for a student's Diploma Programme. Exploration of the nature of knowledge in TOK transcends and links academic subject areas, demonstrating for students the ways in which they can apply their own knowledge with greater awareness and credibility.

The Extended Essay

A required component, the extended essay is an independent, self-directed piece of research, culminating in a 4000-word essay. From the choice of a suitable research question, to the final completion of the 4000-word essay, students must produce their piece within the constraints of time, essay length, and available resources. This component provides an opportunity to engage in an in-depth study of a topic of interest within a chosen subject. Emphasis is placed on the research process, on the appropriate formulation of a research question, on personal engagement in the exploration of the topic, and on communication of ideas and development of argument. It develops the capacity to analyze, synthesize, and evaluate knowledge, with a personal choice of topic from within any subject area. Students are supported and encouraged throughout the research and writing with advice and guidance from a supervisor.

Creativity Action Service

Creativity, action, service (CAS) is a framework for experiential learning and reflection about that learning. CAS is intended to provide experiences for students to develop self-confidence and empathy, and a willingness to help others. The IBO's aim of educating the whole person comes alive in a practical, demonstrable way through CAS. The three elements of CAS are mutually reinforcing. Together, they enable students to recognize that there are many opportunities to learn about life, self, and others, and to inspire confidence, determination, and commitment. Creative and physical activities are particularly important for adolescents and they offer many favorable situations for involvement and enjoyment at a time that is for many young people stressful and uncertain. The service element of CAS is perhaps the most significant of the three, in terms of the development of respect for others, and of responsibility and empathy.

Teacher Role

Because the IBO Curriculum is moderated from the outside of the given school, and the diploma is awarded by the IBO, it is critical that the teachers understand the criteria of the assessments, the goals of the IBO, and the objectives of the given area of study. To meet the needs of the teachers who need to understand the IBO, teacher workshops are given all over the world during the summer and extended breaks. The teacher registers for his or her field, say A1 English, and attends a week long training workshop generally taught by experienced examiners and IBO teachers. Upon successful completion of the workshop, the participants are awarded a certificate.

What is interesting to note is that the IBO rewards candidate works for *personal response* in their externally moderated assessments. What this does is attempt to free the teacher from teaching a template for handling the topic, or from teaching directly to the test. Because one moderator marks the papers for a given school, she can determine quite easily if the answers are too uniform. If they are, the students are marked down for a lack of personal response.

The IBO program demands a high degree of self-motivation from candidates. Many diploma requirements must be completed outside of class, with only general guidance from the classroom teacher. Simply put, the teacher's role is to prepare the candidates for the assessments required by the IBO. The teacher must help students understand the nature of each assessment and the criteria by which it will be graded. This sometimes means conveying and explaining information through lectures or other forms of direct instruction. But more importantly, the teacher must help the students develop the thinking skills necessary to perform the various IBO assessments.

Assessments

Throughout their two year program, IBO Candidates undertake several assessment activities These assessments are divided into two categories: Internal assessment and External assessment.

- ◆ *External assessment*

  These include those activities that are marked by IBO examiners outside the school, and constitute the majority, often seventy percent, of the candidate's overall course grade. For such assessments, it is the classroom teacher's role to prepare the students for exams or guide them in the choice of project topics, but not to grade them. The most significant of the external assessments are two written examinations normally taken at the end of the course. These examinations vary according to the subject, but might include both oral and written responses to questions, or full length essays, and may last from 90 minutes to 3 hours.

However, some courses require candidates to complete projects for external assessment by IBO examiners. Such projects might include essays, visual arts notebooks, or creative writing concerning a work of literature. Typically, students are expected to complete such projects independently, with minimal guidance from the classroom teacher, and little if any class time is to be devoted to these assessments.

- ◆ *Internal assessment*

  While the majority of a candidate's work is marked by outside examiners, a minimum of twenty percent of the student's score comes from Internal Assessment activities that are scored by the classroom teacher. Such activities often include classroom presentations, formal lectures, dramatic performances, role-playing, laboratory experiments, oral commentaries of a literary passage, and oral examinations in the foreign languages.

- ◆ *Moderation*

  Because the IBO must assess work from students in 110 countries, it has developed a system of maintaining consistency in grading practices among classroom teachers and IBO examiners. Moderation occurs on two levels. Certain internal assessments are remarked by IBO examiners, who may alter the student's final score. Likewise, IBO examiners themselves must submit samples of marked papers to be remarked by more experienced chief examiners. Such a system encourages careful assessment of student work and rigorous application of the IBO grading criteria.

◆ *Criterian-based grading system.*

The IBO uses a criterion based grading system rather than normative grading.

Environment

The environment in which the IBO curriculum is implemented is formal in all respects requiring a minimum of 240 hours of classroom instruction for an HL course, and 150 hours for a SL course. Of course, these hours are extended over the two years. The CAS requirement alone is informal and can be met with an average of 3 to 4 hours per week for the 2 years (200 hours or so total).

Although classroom environment varies according to individual teaching styles, the rigorous nature of the IBO program encourages a rather formal classroom environment. Students are expected not only to memorize facts, but must demonstrate synthesis of information, critical and original thinking, and a relevant personal response to what they have learned. In many courses class discussion is as important a means as lecturing in preparing students to respond thoughtfully to questions they might encounter in their final exams. For this reason, discussions remain formal, and students are encouraged to practice articulating their ideas clearly and concisely.

Your Turn

◆ Assuming you did not attend an IBO school, think about what the experience would have been like, and how it might compare to your own high school curriculum.

Summing Up

It is clear from our examination of the ideas of Bruner, Hirsch, Eisner, and Adler that the knowledge-centered curriculum is not merely one of lecture and textbooks, paper and pencil, tests, and grades. Although at those levels when at its most simplistic, it ought not to be that. Yet the purpose remains clear: to learn the canon, however differentially it is described, and to acquire a liberal education. Bruner advocates discovery, inquiry, and group investigation, as well as a balanced approach that includes enactive, iconic, and symbolic learning. Adler advocated a curriculum that uses didactic methods, coaching, and supervised practice, and active participation in discussion and projects. Hirsch, too, argues for balance, going so far as to state that his core knowledge curriculum should probably not account for more than half of the school day.

The knowledge-centered curriculum is an academic curriculum in which students are expected to acquire knowledge of their world as a foundation for adult life. The argument is essentially that there are crucial stages of life in which certain things must be learned or they will never be learned. Childhood and adolescence are times of great learning potential, and these times must not be squandered by dumbing down the curriculum. The academic disciplines represent the core of the curriculum, and the education students receive in the years from kindergarten through twelfth grade should be a liberal education of sufficient breadth, depth, and quality to prepare them not only for university studies but for life in general. This is the worldview of the knowledge-centered advocate. It is a worldview of the liberally educated person who values learning for its own sake, as an end in itself, and not as means of getting jobs and passing exams. As Bruner (1995) noted, "All the standards in the world will not, like a helping hand, achieve the goal of making our multicultural, our threatened society come alive again, not alive just as a competitor in the world's markets, but as a nation worth living in and living for."

8

Parting Thoughts

In her most insightful book, *Raising America: Experts, Parents, and a Century of Advice about Children* (2003), Ann Hulbert notes that throughout the 20th Century, there always existed a tension between expert advocates of "hard" parenting (parent-centered) versus "soft" parenting (child-centered). For every Margaret Mead or Benjamin Spock, it seems there has been a John Watson or James Dobson. The basic argument is over whether parents ought to take a more "naturalistic/laid back" or "directive/interventionist" approach to raising their children. What are parents to think when the experts so clearly disagree? What are educators to think about curricular propriety when the experts so clearly disagree? The purpose of this book is the examination of various theories, models, and exemplars of curriculum. Our examination has made it clear to anyone who might have doubted it, that there is a wide range of opinion regarding curricular propriety. The possibilities, while perhaps not endless, do indeed cover a considerable amount of ground, raising fundamental questions regarding the purposes of school. We can think of the possibilities spread out along a continuum from traditional to experimental, but such a designation does little more than serve as a port of entry. Traditional forms of the curriculum, all of which are in agreement on a pre-planned, adult-directed course of study, do themselves vary when it comes to how students should best spend their time. And experimental forms vary fundamentally in their emphasis on the individual versus the group, over whether the pre-eminent goal of the curriculum is self-realization or societal change, and even the extent to which a curriculum exists. Knowledge is at the heart of any curriculum, but Herbert Spencer's question of what knowledge is of most worth is a matter of contention. Knowledge of history, mathematics, and literature is one thing; knowledge of self and others is quite another. Who decides what students should learn? Is it best for informed adults to plan and manage the learning experience? Or should the student(s) decide what to learn? Who, after all, knows better than the learner? Will students be disadvantaged at some point if they do not cover a systematically planned scope and sequence throughout their school years? These questions will summon different answers depending on one's sense of educational propriety. Finally, is some sort of accommodation possible between complete student interest and a pre-planned curriculum? Can we have the best of all possible worlds? What might a curriculum look like that achieves proper balance among learner, society, and academic knowledge?

If we can agree for purposes of discussion, that there are three ways we know what we know, that is: knowledge received, knowledge discovered, and knowledge constructed, then to what extent can we agree on how much of each is the appropriate mixture? Knowledge received is knowledge gained as a result of being told, by text, teacher, etc. Knowledge discovered is all about finding out for oneself. Knowledge constructed is what happens when learners make meaning of ideas. If knowledge is mainly to be received by learners, then how is the role of the teacher cast? Or if knowledge is mainly a matter of personal and social construction by learners, then what is expected of students and teachers? If knowledge discovered leads to greater "ownership" by the discoverer, then to what extent should a curriculum be discovery oriented? Surely, these questions are as significant as those over whether a curriculum is centered in learner interest, societal change, or academic knowledge.

If we can agree that there are three interests to be served in the daily life of schools: technical, practical, and reflective, then what is the appropriate balance? The technical interest argues for a pre-planned, teacher directed, basic skills approach. The practical interest argues for students working together, moving around, talking to one another about what they are doing, and using a project approach. The reflective interest argues for students and teachers honestly assessing the justice, truth, beauty, and relevance of the experience, for giving students voice and empowerment. What happens when any one of the interests takes over the life world of the classroom, shutting out the others? Each of the interests is strategic in its importance, but unless balance is achieved, the school experience is greatly diminished.

Schools began in ancient times as places set apart from the real world. They purposely did not involve themselves in real world learning because the perception was that a real-world emphasis leads to repetition of what already exists. The theory and practice dichotomy is nothing new. Apprenticeships, not formal education, were thought by the Ancients to be the answer for those who demanded real-world learning. Those interested in and capable of probing the frontiers of knowledge were best off in abstract, theory-laden school settings. The idea that a school ought to provide both abstract and practical experience is largely a twentieth century convention.

We heard and read throughout much of that century and now into this one that a problem with the curriculum is that it is too abstract, artificial, and of little help in equipping students with "life skills." Recently, I heard a state superintendent of schools comment (as a primary reason for testing students to determine to what extent they meet academic standards) that we simply do not know what skills will be needed to compete for jobs in the future. This argument is hardly one of knowledge for its own sake. Neither is it one of student interest nor social activism. It is in fact an argument for social efficiency as determiner of the curriculum. The real world is typically invoked when certain essentialists press the argument for science and mathematics as the best preparation for unknown jobs of the future. People mean different things when they say the curriculum must be relevant to the real world. What ought to be the underlying essential purpose of the curriculum? The arguments tend to fall along lines of self-realization (learner-centered), citizenship and/or jobs (society-centered but with different ends in sight), and knowledge for its own sake (knowledge-centered). Obviously, none of the models we've examined fits any one of these descriptions perfectly. All, finally, are a combination of goal structures. On the other hand, a visit to any classroom, any school, will give the insightful observer definite clues to the priorities. Inevitably, they are given some particular order of importance, and that order is evident in how students and teachers spend the day.

Regardless of what students study and regardless of whether or not they choose what they will study, how do they, how do we, know what they are learning? One solution, popular indeed today, is to test everybody. That solution is faulted by those who contend that standardized tests, no matter how much they claim to test thinking as well as knowledge, tell us very little about meaningful student learning. Another point of view is that the only truly meaningful assessment is self-assessment. Learners should be encouraged to think about and act on what they are learning and should not be subjected to other-directed evaluations of what they know. However we decide to determine what students are learning, we still carry the burden of thinking about whether whatever they are learning is worthwhile.

It is tempting to ask, "does one of the approaches to the curriculum produce greater learning? Do students learn more if they study in a system that emphasizes a certain curriculum?" These questions are difficult to answer for two reasons. The first question is, "do students learn more about what?" A learner-centered curriculum may well produce students who feel a greater sense of empowerment about the choices they make. A society-centered curriculum may encourage and result in more community involvement on the part of students. A knowledge-centered curriculum may produce students who have more academic knowledge. But even these are best guesses. It is not at all unusual for advocates of each perspective to portray other perspectives in the form of caricature. Thus we have the knowledge-centered approach portrayed as facts, facts, facts; the society-centered approach portrayed as anti-authority and rebellious in nature; and learner-centered as hopelessly romantic. Such temptation hardly advances the argument.

A second question is, "to what extent is one school curriculum, however it is configured, better than another at producing measurable long-term differences in achievement, attitude, citizenship, and self-realization?" It is difficult to say because the curriculum is merely one of many variables that contribute to learning outcomes. The celebrated Eight Year Study of the 1930s showed that students who attended progressive schools were as prepared for university academic life as were students who attended traditional schools. The more cynically inclined might say neither approach makes a difference compared to differences in socioeconomic status. There are simply too many confounding variables at work in any given student's life, making it nearly impossible to disentangle the many contributions to a student's formal education and his or her ability to prosper as a learner. A third question is, "does any particular curriculum when compared to others result in a more satisfying experience?" No curriculum can make teachers love children. No curriculum is more motivating or stimulating than any other apart from the quality of the experience. No curriculum is more morally uplifting than any other apart from the honesty, kindness, and dignity with which it is delivered. There probably is no such thing as an estimable curriculum apart from the human elements of how that curriculum is lived. The psychologist Bruno Bettelheim probably had it right when he said that common sense is the characteristic most needed of those who work in school settings. Finally, we must come to terms with the American educational system, a decentralized system, suspicious of federal and even state control and one vested with far more local authority than almost any other system in the world. Therefore, we ought not to be surprised to encounter such a range of ideas of curricular propriety. The exemplars found in these pages are very different one from another. And they are merely samples of what is to be found. No doubt some group is meeting somewhere as you read this, dreaming of an ideal curriculum for the young.

Bibliography

Adler, M. (1984). *The Paideia program: An educational syllabus.* New York: Macmillan.

Adler, M. (1982). *The Paideia proposal.* New York: Macmillan.

Aiken, W. (1942) *The story of the eight year study.* New York: Harper and Brothers.

Alexander, W. (1968). Shaping curriculum: Blueprint for a new school. In U. Unruh & R. Leeper (Eds.), Influence in curriculum change: Papers from a conference sponsored by the ASCD Commission on Current Curriculum Developments, December 1966 (pp. 3–12). Washington, DC: Association for Supervision and Curriculum Development, NBA.

American Association of School Administrators. AASA.org

Anderson, L. (1981). Introduction to instruction and curriculum development. In B. Bloom (Ed.), *All our children learning: A primer for parents, teachers, and other educators* (p. 121–129). New York: McGraw-Hill.

Barrow, R. (1984). *Giving teaching back to teachers: A critical introduction to curriculum theory.* Sussex, UK: Wheatsheaf.

Beane, J. (1995). Curriculum integration and the disciplines of knowledge. *Phi Delta Kappan 76;* 616–622.

Beane, J. (1997). *Curriculum integration: Designing the core of democratic education.* New York: Teachers College Press.

Benne, K. & Muntyan, B. (1951). *Human relations in curriculum change.* New York: Dryden.

Bennet, T. (2001). Reactions to visiting the infant-toddler and preschool centers in Reggio Emilia, Italy. *Early Childhood Research & Practice: An internet journal on the development, care, and education of young children 3;* 1.

Bernstein, E. (1968). "What does a Summerhill old school tie look like?" *Psychology Today 70;* 38–41.

Bestor, A. (1953). *Educational wastelands: The retreat from learning in our public schools.* Urbana: University of Illinois Press.

Bestor, A. (1955). Cited in F. Connelly and D. Clandinin (1988). *Teachers as curriculum planners: Narratives of experience,* (p. 5). New York: Teachers College.

Block, A. (1998). Curriculum as *affichiste*: Popular culture and identity. In W. Pinar (Ed.), *Curriculum: Toward new identities* (p. 325–341). New York: Garland.

Blow, S. (1894). *Symbolic education.* New York: D. Appleton and Company.

Bobbitt, F. (1918). *The curriculum.* Boston: Houghton Mifflin.

Brameld, T. (1955) *Philosophies of education in cultural perspective.* New York: Holt, Rinehart and Winston.

Bruner, J. (1960). *The process of education.* Cambridge, MA: Harvard.

Bruner, J. (1996). *The culture of education.* Cambridge, MA: Harvard.

Bullough, R., Goldstein, S., & Holt, L. (1984). *Human interests in the curriculum: Teaching and learning in a technological society.* New York: Teachers College.

Caswell, H. & Campbell, D. (1935). *Curriculum development.* New York: American Book.

Cay, D. (1966). *Curriculum: Design for learning.* Indianapolis: The Bobbs-Merrill.

Cornbleth, C. (1990). *Curriculum in context.* London: Palmer.

Cremin, L. (Ed.) (1957). *The republic and the school: Horace Mann on the education of free men.* New York: Teachers College Columbia.

Croall, J. (1983). *Neill of Summerhill.* New York: Pantheon.

Crosby, M. (1964). *Curriculum development for elementary schools in a changing society.* Boston: D. C. Heath.

Counts, G. (1932). *Dare the schools build a new social order?* New York: John Day.

de Alba, A., Gonzalez-Gaudino, E., Lankshear, C., & Peters, M. (2000). *Curriculum in the postmodern condition.* New York: Peter Lang.

Dewy, J. (1900). *The school and society.* Chicago: University of Chicago.

Dewey, J. (1913). *Interest and effort in education.* Cambridge, MA: Riverside.

Dewey, J. (1916). *Democracy and education.* New York: Macmillan.

Dewey, J. (1933). *How we think: A restatement of the relation of reflective thinking to the educative process.* Boston: Houghton Mifflin.

Dewey, J. (1938). *Experience and education.* New York: Macmillan.

Dickens, C. (1854, 1961). *Hard times for these times.* New York: New American Library.

Doll, R. (1996). *Curriculum improvement: Decision making and process* (9th ed.). Boston: Allyn and Bacon.

East Tennessee State University Center for Childhood Learning and Development. (n.d.) *The Reggio inspired approach.* Retrieved June 4, 2003, from www.child.etsu.edu.

Eby, F. (1952). *The development of modern education, 2nd edition.* Englewood Cliffs, NJ: Prentice-Hall, Inc.

Edmiaston, R. & Fitzgerald, L. (2000). How Reggio Emilia encourages inclusion. *Educational Leadership*, 58 (1), 66–69.

Edwards, C. (2002). Three approaches from Europe: Waldorf, Montessori, and Reggio Emilia. *Early Childhood Research & Practice: An internet journal on the development, care, and education of young children*, 4 (1). Retrieved May, 9, 2003 from www.ecrp.uiuc.edu.

Eisner, E. (Ed.) (1984). *Learning and teaching the ways of knowing*. Chicago: National Society for the Study of Education.

Ellis, A., & Glenn, A. (1977). "The effects of real and contrived problem solving on economic learning." *Journal of Economic Education 8*(2).

Foshay, A. (1968). Shaping curriculum: The decade ahead. In G. Unruh & R. Leeper (Eds.), *Influence in curriculum change: Papers from a conference sponsored by the ASCD Commission on Current curriculum Developments, December, 1966* (pp. 3–12).Washington, DC: Association for Supervision and Curriculum Development, NEA.

Foxfire Fund (n.d.). *An educator's guide to schoolwide reform*. Retrieved June 1, 2003 from www.aasa.org.

Freire, P. (1970). *A pedagogy of the oppressed*. New York: Continuum.

Fukuyama, F. (1995). *Trust: The social virtues and the creation of prosperity*. London: Hamish Hamilton.

Gay, O. (1990). *Achieving educational equality through curriculum desegregation*. Phi Delta Kappan 72; 130.

Gideonse, H. (1968). Curriculum realities. In E. Short & G. Marconnit (Eds.), *Contemporary thought on public school curriculum* (pp. 35 1–356). Dubuque, IA: W. C. Brown.

Good, C. (1973). *Dictionary of education* (3d ed.). New York: McGraw-Hill.

Goodlad, J. (1984). *A place called school*. New York: McGraw-Hill.

Grundy, S. (1987). *Curriculum: Product or praxis?* London, UK: Palmer.

Hass, G. (1987). *Curriculum planning: A new approach* (5th ed.). Boston: Allyn and Bacon.

Hirsch, E. D. Jr. (1987). *Cultural literacy: What every American needs to know*. Boston: Houghton Mifflin.

Hirsch, E. D. Jr. (1999). *The schools we need and why we don't have them*. New York: Anchor Books.

Hirsch, E. D. Jr. (2001). You can always look it up—or can you? *Common Knowledge 13*; 2–3.

Hopkins, L. T. (1941). *Interaction: The democratic process*. Boston: D. C. Heath.

Hulbert, A. (2003). *Raising America: Experts, parents, and a century of advice about children*. New York: Alfred Knopf.

Hutchins, R. (1952). *The great conversation: The substance of a liberal education*. Chicago: Encyclopaedia Britannica.

Hutchins, R. (1953). *The conflict in education*. New York: Harper.

Jenkins, D. & Shipman, M. (1996). *Curriculum: An introduction*. London, UK: Open Books.

Joseph, P. (2000). Conceptualizing curriculum. In P. Joseph, S. Bravmann, M. Windschitl, B. Mike, & N. Green (Eds.), *Cultures of curriculum* (pp. 1–14). Mahwah, NJ: Lawrence Erlbaum.

Johnson, M. (1967). Definitions and models in curriculum theory. *Educational Theory* 1; 127–140.

Katz, L., & Chard, S. (1996). *The contribution of documentation to the quality of early childhood education.* Champaign, IL: ERIC Clearinghouse on Elementary and Early Childhood Education, No. EDO-PS-96-2.

Kerr, J. (Ed.). (1968). *Changing the curriculum.* London, UK: University of London.

Kilpatrick, W. (1918). The project method. *Teachers College Record.*

Knowles, J. (1981). *Peace breaks out.* New York: Bantam.

Kugelmass, J. (1995). Educating children with learning disabilities in Foxfire classrooms. *Journal of Learning Disabilities* 28; 9.

Kyte, G. (1957). *The elementary school teacher at work.* New York: Dryden.

Lee, J. & Lee, D. (1950). *The child and his curriculum* (2nd ed.). New York: Appleton-Century Crofts.

Logan, L., & Logan, V. (1961). *Teaching the elementary school child.* Boston: Houghton Mifflin.

Marsh, C., & Stafford, K. (1984). *Curriculum: Australian practices and issues.* Sydney: McGraw- Hill.

McCombs, B. & Whisler, J. (1997). *The learner-centered classroom and school: Strategies for increasing student motivation and achievement.* San Francisco: Jossey-Bass.

Neagley, R. L., & Evans, N. D. (1967). *Handbook for effective curriculum development.* Englewood Cliffs, NJ: Prentice-Hall.

Neill, A. (1917). *A domine dismissed.* London: Herbert Jenkins.

Neill, A. (1970). *Summerhill: For and against.* New York: Hart.

New, R. (1993). *Reggio Emilia: Some lessons for U.S. educators.* Champaign, IL: ERIC Clearinghouse on Elementary and Early Childhood Education, No. EDO-PS-93-3.

New, R. (2000). *Reggio Emilia: Catalyst for change and conversation.* Champaign, IL: ERIC Clearinghouse on Elementary and Early Childhood Education, No. EDO-PS-00-15.

Oliva, P. (1982). *Developing the curriculum.* Boston: Little, Brown.

Oliva, P. (1997). *Developing the curriculum* (4th ed.). New York: Longman.

Oliver, A. (1968). What is the meaning of "Curriculum"? In E. Short & G. Marconnit (Eds.), *Contemporary thought on public school curriculum* (pp. 3–9). Dubuque, IA: W. C. Brown.

Olmstead, K. (1989). *Touching the past, en route to the future: Cultural journalism in the curriculum of rural schools.* Charleston, WV: ERIC Clearinghouse on Rural Education Small Schools, No. ED308057.

Parkay, F. & Hass, G. (2000). *Curriculum planning: A contemporary approach.* Boston: Allyn & Bacon.

Peterson, A. (2003). *Schools across frontiers: The story of the International Baccalaureate and the United World Colleges.* New York: Open Court Publishers.

Pratt, D. (1980). *Curriculum: Design and development.* New York: Harcourt, Brace Jovanovich.

Prescott, D. (1957). *The child in educative process.* New York: McGraw-Hill.

Quintilian. (1987) *Quintilian on the teaching of speaking and writing.* Carbonale, IL: Southern Illinois University Press.

Ragan, W. B. (1960). *Modern elementary curriculum* (rev. ed.). New York: Henry Holt.

Ravitch, D. (2000*). Left back: A century of school reforms.* New York: Simon and Schuster.

Roberts, T. & Billings, L. (1999). T*he power of Paideia schools: Defining lives through learning.* Alexandria, VA: ASCD.

Rogers, C. (1969). *Freedom to learn.* Columbus, OH: Charles E. Merrill.

Rogers, C., & Freiberg, J. (1994). *Freedom to learn* (3d ed.). New York: Merrill.

Rousseau, J. (1762/1978). *The social contract, or principles of political right.* (J. Masters, Trans.). New York: St. Martin.

Saylor, J. G., Alexander, W., & Lewis, A. (1980). *Curriculum planning for better teaching and learning* (4th ed.). New York: Holt, Rinehart and Winston.

Sergiovanni, T. (1994). *Building community in schools.* San Francisco: Jossey-Bass.

Smith, B. O., Stanley, W. O., & Shores, J. H. (1957). *Fundamentals of curriculum development* (rev. ed.). Yonkers on Hudson, NY: World Book.

Sowards, G. W., & Scobey, M. (1962). *The changing curriculum and the elementary teacher.* Belmont, CA: Wadsworth.

Spencer, H. (1896). *Education: Intellectual, moral, and physical.* New York: D. Appleton.

Starnes, B. (1999). *The Foxfire approach to teaching and learning: John Dewey, experiential learning and the core practices.* Charleston, WV: ERIC Clearinghouse on Rural Education and Small Schools, No. ED426826.

Stenhouse, L. (1975). *An introduction of curriculum research and development.* London, UK: Heinemann.

Taba, H. (1962). *Curriculum development: Theory and practice.* New York: Harcourt, Brace, Jovanovich.

Tanner, D., & Tanner, L. (1995). *Curriculum development: Theory into practice* (3d ed.). New York: Merrill.

Walberg, H. (1984). Improving the productivity of America's schools. *Educational Leadership,* 41(8); 19–27.

Weiner, B. (1995). *Judgments of responsibility: A foundation for a theory of social conduct.* New York: Guilford.

Wiles, J., & Bondi, J. (1993). *Curriculum development: A guide to practice* (4th ed.). New York: Merrill.

Whitehead, A. (1929, 1967). *The aims of education and other essays.* New York: The Free Press.

Wragg, B. C. (1997). *The cubic curriculum.* London, UK: Routledge.

Index

Hopkins, T., 5
Hulbert, A., 149, 155
Hutchins, Robert, 102–103, 155
IBO model, 140
IBO principles, 139
independent study, 54
inquiry, 59–60
instruction, 56
instructional model, Bruner's, 99
integrated studies, 30, 76–77
interest centers, 46–47, 57–58
International Baccalaureate Diploma
    Programme, 138–146
Isaacs, Susan, 47
Jenkins, R., 155
Joseph, P., 155
Katz, L., 65, 156
Kerr, J., 156
key ideas, 115
Kilpatrick, William, 31
kindergarten, 3, 29
knowledge, interpretive nature of,
    143
knowledge, purposes of, 149–152
Knowles, John, 25
Kugelmass, J., 81, 156
Kyte, J., 156
laboratory schools, 30
Lankshear, C., 7
Latin Grammar School, 109
leadership, schoolwide, 136
learning environment, 48
Lee, D., 156
Lee, J., 156
Lewis, A., 157
liberal education, 94–96
life experience education, 30
life problems, 71
life skills, 151
locus of control, 49
Logan, L., 156
Logan, V., 156

Malaguzzi, L., 62, 64–65
Malting House School, 47
Man: A Course of Study, 98–99
Mann, Horace, 18, 102, 121
manufacturing unit, 85
Marsh, C., 6
Maslow, Abraham, 41, 48
McCombs, B., 39
Mead, Margaret, 149
mixed-age learning, 53
model, defined, xii
multiple intelligences theory, 100,
Muntyan, B., 153
Nader, Ralph, 87
National Council of Teachers of
    Mathematics, 96, 107
National Education Association, 31
National Paideia Center, 131–132,
    137
National Science Foundation, 96
National Society for the Study of
    Education, 100
nature trails unit, 86
Neagley, R., 156
Neill, A.S., 9, 44–45, 55
New, R., 63
Newton, Isaac, 116
nurturer, teacher as, 60–61
Oliva, P., 4, 156
Oliver, A., 156
Olmstead, K., 81, 83, 156
open education, 43–44
pageants, 73
Paideia Curriculum, 131–137
Paideia principles, 132–133
Paideia Proposal, 102
Paideia teaching methods, 134
Parkay, F., 156
Parker, Colonel Francis, 31
pedestrian crossings unit, 88, 89
perennialism, 109–114
perennialist paradigm, 128–130

performing arts, 59
Pestalozzi, Johann, 29
Peters, M., 7
Peterson, A., 139, 157
philosophy, defined, xii
Piaget, Jean, 33, 48, 77
Plato, xvi, 47, 61, 128
pluralism, 22–23
Pratt, D., 157
Prescott, D., 157
problem solving, 59–60, 71
Process of Education, The, 100
progressive curriculum, elements of, 34
Progressive Education Association, 32
progressive movement, 29–36
project learning, 30
project method, 31
Quintilian, 29, 47, 49, 52
Ragan, W., 5, 157
Ravitch, Diane, 91, 93, 95, 105
real-world problems, 71
recess, 60
Reggio Emilia, 62–65
Reggio Emilia, principles of, 63
relationships, 55
Rickover, Hyman, 123
Roberts, T., 131, 157
Rogers, Carl, 43, 45
romantic movement, 3
Rousseau, Jean-Jacques, 29, 33–34, 42
Rugg, Harold, 31
Saylor, A., 157
schedule, EECES, 58–59
schooling, goals of, xiv
Scobey, M., 157
self in group context, 74
self-actualization, 41
self-direction, 48
self-realization, 41
seminars, 135

Sergiovanni, T., 69
Seven Cardinal Principles, 113
Shipman, M., 155
Shores, J., 157
skills sessions, 87
skills, 20
Smith, B., 157
societal issues, 71
society-centered curriculum, keys to, 72
Socratic dialogue, 129, 135
soft-drink design unit, 85
Sowards, G., 157
Spencer, Herbert, 18, 19, 149–150
spiral curriculum, 116
Spock, Benjamin, 149
St. Johns College, 129
Stafford, K., 6
standardized tests, 151
Stanley, W., w57
Starnes, B., 81, 82, 157
Stenhouse, L., 157
structure of disciplines, 115–116
student role, 35, 121, 136
study, 56
Sudbury Schools, 52–55
Sudbury Valley School, 52
Summerhill School, 44–45
syntactic complexity, 49
systems theory, 13
Taba, H., 4
Tanner, D., 5
Tanner, L., 5
teachable moment, 87
teacher role, 75–76, 128, 135–136, 144
television viewing, 17
textbook adoptions, 119
textbooks, 96–98
Theory of Knowledge (IBO), 142–143
theory, defined, xii

third teacher, 64
Thurber, James, 15
Tolkien, J.R.R., 3
traffic flow unit, 86
trust, 21–22
trust, 45
Unified Science and Mathematics for
  Elementary Schools, 85–90
values, 19–20
Walberg, H., 44
Watson, John, 149
Ways of Knowing 100
weather predictions unit, 86
Weiner, B., 21, 157
Whisler, J., 39
Whitehead, A.N., 66–67, 116
Wigginton, E., 81
Wiles, J., 158
Wragg, B., 158